# *I See You with My Heart*

### Jean Posusta

ISBN 978-1-64515-011-4 (paperback)
ISBN 978-1-64515-012-1 (digital)

Christian Faith Publishing, Inc.
832 Park Avenue
Meadville, PA 16335
www.christianfaithpublishing.com

Printed in the United States of America

Oh. So much insight into the walk of a family through the suffering of brain cancer in a loved one. I feel like I walked through their door and experienced the emotions each of the characters felt. From hilarious irreverence to an intense demonstration of faith to recovery from grief.

—Corinne McGrew, Paralegal

So much touched my heart, that crying made it hard to read. I was there with the doctor, at the bar with them, standing in their kitchen; moved to experiencing their pain, love, and joy.

—Dr. V. Burford, Clinical Therapist

Good to the last drop. Characters well-built and the story both breaks your heart and mends it.

—Betti Henrichs

For my mom

# I'm Going to Become a Nun (~~Not~~)

NEARLY DID IT. I sat in the conclave-like chapel/classroom, listening first to Sister Teresa Ann's beatific intros then first-year novice Berleena stood as she spoke behind the part-time-altar podium. They each coerced St. Catherine's novice aspirant candidates for the cloistered program. Sister Teresa Ann had been married before nunhood! Her mere presence demanded venerated ecclesiastical awe. I was thinking of cum.

Behind the lector, in front of the huge stained-glass window rainbowing the sun's rays, was an eight-foot alabaster white statue of the Immaculate Mary. Someone left-brained, I surmised, put a baby blue light bulb in the canister light that illuminated her, casting a shadow that outsized the very statue on the shiny marble floor. The combination of sun through the stained glass and blue cast of light created not only a rainbow halo, but an obscure haze that made one think they were in heaven. That's exactly the premeditating thought I would have after leaving my temporal life and becoming a nun—me, bathed in blue illumination, serene and baked in a pearlescent aura, larger than life, and knowing that I had procured my place in heaven by joining the convent.

A confraternity of black wimbled faces stared out between the statue's blue aura and Sister Teresa Ann.

A walking book of rules and a sage, Sister Teresa Ann dourly read to us:

"Admission to a convent has several guidelines. Foremost, a candidate must have a vocation. A vocation to religious life is dependent on three things: the candidate's personal fitness spiritually, mentally and physically; the desire of the candidate to enter into religious life; and finally, the Church's invitation to the individual to enter into that way of life.

...Usually, a candidate must be healthy, sound of body and mind, a Catholic of good standing, have no outside debts or responsibilities (such as taking care of a parent or child, be married, etc.) Even if obstacles arise from the above, the candidate can seek a dispensation from her local archbishop in order to proceed though whether it is granted or not is at the discretion of the archbishop. The candidate can then either approach her local parish priest and request assistance in pursuing a vocation to a convent, or she can go directly to a convent to speak with the abbess there about entry. Most convents will give potential candidates a few forms to fill out and require several character witnesses and an interview; it's not unlike applying for a position in a company.

...From the moment of their glorious installation mass..." She went on.

As I sat there in my glorious imagination, I wondered what the gal in the seat just in front of me had for breakfast. I could see her lap over the back of the pew. There, on a black linen skirt pleat, was this yuck—this oatmeal-like glob/stain on the skirt of her dress. Otherwise she looked impeccably kempt (as opposed to unkempt). I wondered why she is wearing black—is she kissy-facing the nuns? I know Jewish girls like to wear pink to their bat mitzvahs, but was there criterion for clothing today?

See, I knew in that moment I was not going to marry God. If I can't concentrate with enough initial attention to pay due homage to a nun's speech during just the introduction to the novicery, there was no way I could conjure up the required devoutness to endure nunnery life. Oh for the love of God, what was I thinking?

"What is holiness?" Prefect Sister Teresa Ann posed to the congregation gathered for the lecture.

Is that rhetorical? Does she want us to answer her?

Almost all of us fidgeted, careful to not make eye contact with her yet look pretentiously pious. Was she, from the pulpit, requiring us to answer? Not a one of us yet knew the protocol for a Novice Aspirant Candidates (the NAC conference) introduction lecture. Still as the wooden pew, I sat. As did *all* the others. Sister Teresa Ann went on with her own answer. A soft "whew" breathed through the aspirants.

Sister Teresa Ann then began to fill us in on the many hoops and tests, and questioning forays ahead of us, to even become a "candidate" to become a novice. We were actually only a contemplative nun at this point, heading into the charism of religious life. *Why didn't they just use the word charm?* I wondered.

All I could think of was the cat puke or whatever was on the black linen pleat in front of me. Will lightning strike this corpus delicti right here in this pew? Where's my sanctified piety for church?

I should have known. When I filled out St. Catherine's application, one of my predominant thoughts was that I would finally know what the cloistered dwellers wore underneath their habits. Good grief, if that is my curiosity factor, where was I going to find the prayerfulness and the humility and the charm-filled humanitarianism necessary to be a Sister to the Lord? I believe I was more curious than interested in learning the rituals of convent life than what holiness meant to me. So as I sat there wondering about the oatmeal stain, a new revelation did actually come to me—get out.

Perhaps I had kidded myself, "deviated from my principals" as the Good Book says, but I believed I had a calling. I thought I was doing what Mom—herself so pious—wanted her children to do. She had always told us when we did something selfless that, "I can see the Christ in you." And therefore, I wanted her to see what I was doing from heaven now. I had been undecided about my direction in life and then I had the supposed calling. So I signed up for the Sister Teresa Ann's introductory class to begin fulfilling my calling. However, the oatmeal stain was the end of the aspirant in me.

Did you know that habits are usually one piece of cloth, representative of Jesus's woven covering? There I go, thinking about clothes. Hm. I wonder about myself. Is that a doubt in my mind? Oh, dear. Is there a career in clothing design for ministerial staff? I would be good at that!

"A postulant must have a vocation." Sister Teresa Ann went on. Well, I thought I did have a vocation… I wanted to be a nun! Well, I guess I failed the first question. Wonder if I could get special dispensation for that? Next you have to be of good physical fitness and sound mind. The dispensation question arose again.

A postulant…my mind flickered again, envisioning a *postulant* in the stiff white flying nun head gear, like that Australian domed arena or a dog's bite-protective collar.

I hated to have to go home and tell my sisters that I chickened out on God. Yet, I had been so sure at the time I got the calling that I was destined to be consecrated to God. It wasn't exactly like Samson being told not to cut his hair or Elijah's or Joseph's magnanimous technicolored cloaks, standing out as beloved in that manner.

By now, I had convinced myself that the goo on the black pleat in the pew just ahead was cum, and my imagination had taken me to any scene that would bring that girl here rushing, so soon after consummating.

# The Spawning of the Calling

ONE SATURDAY IN APRIL of this year, I was mentally praying while I was cleaning out dad's old '65 Dodge which we kept in our back garage in fond memory, and I found the pewter St. Christopher magnet that used to adorn our dashboard lying in the glove compartment. It was in our Dodge since the Catholic Church, a decade or six ago in 1969, venerated him from Martryology and ousted that now fictitious character, St. Christopher, as the patron saint of travelers. As I thrust my hand in to get the magnetic figure of St. Chris from the depths of the glove compartment, I accidentally pierced the center of my palm, making a Jesus-like mark with a pen which was sticking up. It didn't hurt at all, but blood came instantly, enough for me to think about getting a Band-Aid. I reached for the door, kind of underhanded from my contorted-glove-box-cleaning position, to get out of the car. I managed instead to lock all the car doors. As I turned my injured hand in a crooked manner to unlatch the door, I saw that the bleeding diminished completely, and the puncture wound seemed to have disappeared, almost like the blood was sucked back under my skin. A shiver passed through my entire body sitting there. I looked at the palm of my hand again. Hmm.

So back to cleaning, I reached again more carefully into the cubby for the St. Christopher magnet. A perfect cross of sunshine appeared smack in the middle of the round coin like St. Chris's—the radiant glow on the crucifix was to Hollywood-film-like perfection. A reflection off the chrome of a truck bumper pulling in the driveway right behind Dad's Dodge had caused the mirrored crucifix image. The bumper belonged to Gainan's florist truck delivering yellow roses for us, the O'Brien sisters—Ceci, Clarey, and me, Margo.

The florist brought yellow roses for the O'Brien sisters from Barry. We three, my two sisters Clarey, Ceci, and I, Margo, had meticulously cleaned his bachelor apartment yesterday. Yellow and pink miniature roses, symbols of friendship and thanks consecutively, were his way of showering us with appreciation.

Ironically, today I had just finished making a Christian novena. A novena is the Catholic equivalent of studying for a midterm—praying lots of rosaries during nine days of devotion. I was praying the final prayer of the novena as I now cleaned Dad's Dodge. I felt I needed to pray about my future, maybe needed to offer some extra prayers, so I was making a novena, a trillion prayers—well actually twenty-seven days of saying the rosary. It took days, even weeks, to help with my decision about joining the Novice program at St. Catherine's—days full of prayer, prayer, Hail Marys. The pen piercing happened after the last "amen." No lie. And then to complete the Novena, one says twenty-seven more days of rosaries in thanks. Now here is the strange part that I am sure an old wife added to the original 1810 tale: at the end of the first set of prayers, a rose will show itself to you in an unplanned manner.

And then the roses arrived from Gainan's Florals. If you are exposed to Catholicism at all, you have probably heard about our novenas. If Mary has heard you saying all these prayers for a certain cause, you will see a rose in the next forty-eight hours. As an aside, I just want to say that I never heard of a man making a novena.

So today, looking at the oatmeal stain and thinking about the blue light bulb behind the bisque statue of Mary and totally not concentrating on why I came here—to possibly enter the novice program, Mom's dream for her child.

Mom's dream. Not mine. I shivered. Another personal revelation.

My pen stopped in the middle of an answer on the novice pre-commitment application. I drifted off to wonder about living a life without sex and that contemplation took me again to wondering again about nuns' underwear. I should have known right then. I don't think that was a normal brain drift for someone committing to a promise-myself-to-God novice program!

Anyway, I re-examined my intentions, replaying the calling moment while I had been cleaning the Dodge. And the fact that the former Young Christian Women Sodality president in my Mom *really* wanted one of her girls to become a nun. I had had this calling—the sun's reflection on St. Christopher's metal, my personal Jesus-like palm piercing, the roses at the end of the novena, and Mom's dream. Until this moment of the Novice Introduction Service, it had been all consumptive—decision made. I was of age, holding a college degree that needed to make me money. I needed a career. And we had a convent in town. Mom had prayed hard, she often told us, that her children would grow up good Christians and matriculate into Catholic service. Her voice, the numbing cantor-like humming of her spoken rosaries still echoed in my head and compelled my honesty and guided my spirituality. I was so sure I had chosen the correct vocational path, this aspirant to be a candidate to be a novice to be a nun. And I had a deep sense of love imbued for God. All the intentions necessary to join a convent, right?

And I had loved being an altar girl, carrying that heavy red book from side to side of the tabernacle and I got to help wash Father's hands and saw Father's belly as he changed into his celestial cassock garments. That was worth extra points here, right? I told no one what I saw inside the sacristy. I could be trusted with all church-owned items.

When the Benedictine Sisters of Perpetual Adoration invited single women who were considering religious life to a monastic experience at the monastery along the Musselshell River, I jumped on the chance. It was a fantastic weekend, full of food and prayer and time alone together. Though five of the seven of us who broke away from a silence period skinny dipped in the Musselshell, all in all, I was pious most of the three days. It was held at the hand-carved rustic log cabins a distance back in the woods near Labina, which we quickly coined Labia in the car on the way, ever to be remembered as that.

The oatmeal/cat puke/cum, though, was the turning point. Sitting in the novice introductory preapplication class, tears came out of my eyes. Tears—no, not appropriately for the loss of civilian life style, or tears for joy for the love I could find in being closer to Christ. At first, I assumed my unelicited tears were due to a strong emotional revelation—an opening of my soul to God's invitation to join the cloister. Was my heart open to his tug at me, little Margo O'Brien? Or was it "Get the hell out of here" tears of fear monopolizing my feelings? The tears ran down my cheeks, and nose rain began to run just as freely down my face as the teardrops, conjoined like a fork in a stream down my chin.

I blew. Quite loudly, actually, for being in church. Instantly, I felt cleansed and light, like a crane just lifted a baby grand off my chest. Now I could only concentrate on where the doors were in the chapel/lecture hall/classroom, the whereabouts of my car keys, and which road would have the least traffic at 10:09 a.m. on Saturday. Nine minutes in was all. I realized what the emotional revelation and tears were about. Get out! This is wrong! Wrong decision to come today, Margo. Not for you. I was not listening to a word the aspirant to be a candidate to be a novice to be a nun questionnaire prompter said.

# *Tripod*

I OPENED THE GREEN door on our three O'Brien sisters'
cute little bungalow home twenty minutes later.

Clarey met me all bright eyed with a candled frosted
cupcake at the front door to celebrate my supposed "new
birth." "You're back soon!" she spoke surprisingly. Ceci
offered me a beer holding a can of Coors Light up in the air
behind Clarey. My ashen skin and the disappointed look
on my face told them everything. I got a hug. They were
both up with arms around me before I was all the way in
the room—the tripod hug. I flash back to a first hug like
this, with play clothes and can cans. We were tight.

Clarey sighed for me. "If it were meant to be, it will still
happen. Being together is most important to us three. The
moment of deciding to change will come again if it's meant
to be. Remember how Mom always said, 'Do not give up
what you want most for what you want at the moment'?
That was a moment of your life and you learned from it.
It's okay. And this too will pass, Margo."

Our tripod. A friend once coined when we did the
routine stance, the "tripod hug." Once other friends had to
wait outside for Ceci before leaving on their trip to climb
icebergs in Canada. The friend told them, "They're in the
tripod hug. They'll be five minutes." So that was it. A phrase

now ad Infinium. The support of our tripod sure came in handy many times when any one of the three of us, my two sisters and me, didn't think we could stand on our own two feet emotionally or physically—like right now.

Like when Clarey broke her leg—it was like all three of us broke a leg—we fussed over the cast, helped to itch down inside the cast, were there for the break of the leg and the finale, sawing off the cast. There was never a one-person event for any of us. We celebrated each other's goodness and cried together over heartbreaks and hurts. I think the tripod was formed long before we were birthed.

Ceci took photography class, came home and taught us. Clarey went to prom with Ceci's purse, and my baby tooth in her locket. We sat down together to open report cards for me. We would get our stories a bit mixed up when we retold them because we are so close, we forget who did what for real—that close.

# Sisters of a Different Clan

BELIEVE IT OR NOT, Ceci was the strongest with her support that night. My beer-loving—perhaps alcoholic—fantastic but somewhat rebellious Ceci. She logically told me, "It just wasn't meant to be. No worries. Nobody died."

She was like that—very practical, no pundits, totally supportive, and strong. I could count on her, always and forever.

When Ceci chose to, she attended the Catholic church. Otherwise she bounced to the Presbyterians, the Four Squares, Baptists, or whoever had a good band on a Sunday. She was a great spiritual follower, but sometimes for months or a year, she was a "CEO," as they say, attending "Christmas and Easter Only" and weddings at the Catholic church. I knew she always prayed. She had the Spirit-filled life walking with patience, love, truth, sincerity, and prayer; believed God created babies, caused the rain, carries dead people to heaven and makes the trees. That wasn't it. She just didn't agree with the Catholic church rote conduct of their worship. When she got fed up with a tithing sermon or liturgical planning, she would just quit attending until her strong love for God and belief in common worship pulled her back to worship in a congregation. She always lived in spirituality, no question about that, but not exactly a born-again canonical attendee.

The rest of the time, she worked as a teacher at Harrington High in the Commonwealth School District, and well, "played with friends," even at her grown-up age of twenty-eight. Oh, and she loved to drink. I thought twenty-seven was the cut-off age to continue to drink with friends on all occasions, you know. Just like at thirty-five, you could no longer be a prostitute. Someone in whom I had put great regard had told me those rules-of-life factoids.

I was the youngest, and Clarey, the oldest—the tripod's other legs. Ceci wouldn't be a nun either, we knew.

I couldn't really call Ceci an alcoholic out loud. Cec was the most well-rounded person I knew. She added the blossoms and fruit to my life. Notoriously fun loving, always with a gregarious story or a hilarious joke to tease you, always involving you, smart, valedictorian Ceci "just like our dad", others told us. She was all most people aspire to be. She had already been a zillion places around the world as an exchange student and with her college friends, every summer experiencing something wonderful with a group throughout and since high school. She had climbed the summit of Lhotse in Nepal, shook the hands of two presidents, attended every concert and musical within 100 miles, had her own scuba set with air lines, and she ate sushi at home. I call that well rounded.

She made the most of her summers off and our inheritance since our parents died. Their insurance plan and Dad's company had left us "well-off". Clarey and I were busy with hometown events and school and neighbors and church contentedly.

Ceci was just one of those people who wanted to do everything life had to offer—to "go around twice, not just go around once" as she called it. She was a graduate in solo skydiving, drove a diver propulsion vehicle in the Indian Ocean off Asian shores, gave golf instructions, ushered folks to seats at the American Cup, and spent a summer in Alaska at the Geophysical Institute of Fairbanks.

She was a CARP, Certified All Round Person. Clarey had given her a plaque one Christmas that declared it so. Cec "lived life large" as they put it.

"Oh, good! I couldn't have stood it if you were cloistered from me," Ceci said, "Not for a day or a month. Who would I talk about sex with?" She always knew how to lighten a heavy moment. In that sentence, I was reaffirmed. It was okay that I was not going to join the convent. She made it okay. After all, she looked the most like our mom of any of the three of us girls, and I needed a sign from my pious mother's spirit that it was okay that I wasn't joining the convent. Ceci's sideways nod, one eyebrow in a quick up and down—so like Mom would have done—gave me the conversive calming I needed.

Clarey, our eldest family member now, didn't show her disappointment, but I knew she held the same hopes as Mom had— for one of us siblings to demonstrate their ubiquitous fervor for God first, by vocation and throughout her life. But I also knew it was okay with Clarey that I didn't stay for the novice lecture.

"It wasn't meant to be. Your wonderful talents and personality will have to be shared in different ways, that's all. I'm just sorry for the cloistered people, that they don't get to have you. I do!" Again, all the love that I needed to hear.

I was a dabbler. I tried this. I hung with this clique. I tried my best at cooking, baking, skiing, painting, wood work, sports—you name it—but never found the talents within. Perhaps joining a convent had just been another dabble.

Clarey had a career. She seemed to be motivated and inspired and wonderful. She was a perfect example of a woman set out to live well and taking all the right roads to sainthood.

I didn't feel I failed, I just hadn't found my niche *yet*. Ceci seemed to have a niche in everything. Maybe I would just follow her footsteps, time will tell.

# More Ceci

WE WORRIED TOGETHER ABOUT Ceci, Clarey and I. While Ceci was living the epitome of what most folks think about when they hope for a fun and fruitful life, she had added an overabundance of beer according to our opinions. While she kept her functionality in check most days, there were some nights, some days, some events where she drank to the edge.

Neither of us voiced it, but I sensed in Clarey (and I know she sensed in me) that we hated that—the drinking.

Ceci managed to keep her job at Harrington High School in spite of herself. She often drank week nights, closed the bars on weekends, and went to work just short of still reeking of booze. Her alcohol level had to be questionable on campus some days. We should have bought stock in Wrigley's Doublemint. There was the ever-present Doublemint gum, like eight packs in her car, her teacher's desk, her bedroom, by the TV, next to the bathroom sink—everywhere. Funny thing was, Clarey and I didn't really consider Ceci to have a problem she couldn't control. We just wondered about it. But we entertained the thought that, that much drinking could harm her. You know, now that she was twenty-eight. Ceci seemed to leave beer alone sometimes for months, and we would get all hopeful, but when she wanted to drink, she did so again with seemingly more gusto. Just like her Catholic church attendance. Clarey even did a quiz in *Health* magazine, "Is Your Relative Bipolar"? Nope, that wasn't an issue. It was just Ceci's personality quirks.

Students and faculty alike loved her. Her pretended non-pompous grandiloquence entertained. She knew so much from her pursuit of firsthand experience and travels including ethnographic studies that science was like first nature to her. The kids probably never realized she was teaching from a textbook because she was so tactile with their education. One early day of Harrington High's fall semester, she prepared an arc of electricity (not harmful) over the doorway, so that every student's hair immediately went straight up upon entering the door. Ceci's own pur- posefully-worn afghan sweater prickled! She slipped some tiny plastic toys in the cadavers overnight when the kids were in her Biology's curriculum phase to dissect frogs. She harvested pigeons from what she said were duck eggs, teaching a lesson not to believe everything everyone tells you, and to ask questions about what you are working with. Lessons like that—practical application. She was always drinking vinegar at home—only after she threw in some baking soda to boil it over. She told people it was her witch's brew.

Clarey and I should have faced the underlying truth. She was an alcoholic. But we, nor Ceci, could acknowledge it aloud. They never had a test for it in *Health* magazine. It would be inconceivable, too humiliating, and shameful for an O'Brien to have an uncontrollable addiction.

Barry Best, the rose bouquet giver, was Ceci's best friend. He could call and whisper one word to Ceci in the phone, "Halo." Not "hello," but "Halo." It meant "Meet me at O'Malley's Tap." "Halo" terminology was a word-play vernacularly used, being they were going where a church key opened the fun, or a beer can opener would open the can—at a bar owned by another Tom O'Malley, who had children, not the Tom O'Malley who was our priest. O'Malley's tap was usually where they both got "fuzz-headed" from drinking.

> You get your halo on,
> if you drink it gone,
> with Father, Father Tom

It was a sing-song sentence when they said it. Applying cutesy names to people was a signature quirky vernacular in their friendship. Father Tom at church was also Tom O'Malley. It was an inside joke. Guess you had to be there back some years ago during a drinking session, when they laughed uproariously over their clever greeting—"halo." Now with her at twenty-eight, I didn't think the rote as funny as when I heard it then. "Prostitutes and drunks have to quit at some age" still in my thinking.

Irish folk predominantly filled our neck of the town of Harrington. St. Catherine's parish priest of ten years shared the same name—Father Thomas O'Malley with Tom O'Malley, the bartender at the tap. It was a question as to which received the greater homage. And bartender Tom was dad to twins, thus coined "Father Tom." Plus bartender Tom claimed to own a relic of Sr. Faustina, two threads of cloth in a glass-covered medal, about half an inch in diameter on display in the bar. Talk about sacrilegious!

These O'Malleys also were cousins—you know, my cousin Tom and my other cousin, Tom? Ceci and Barry thought that the coincidence of names was pretty funny. They thought everything was funny, the two of them. Together, they laughed at life's quirks so much, everyone looked to them to lighten our moments. You couldn't spend five minutes with either without smiling over a pun, a story, or a trick they pulled. And they gave everyone a fun nickname, like you were to be a forever friend of theirs, and would yell your nickname out the car window if they saw you on the street—they were that kind of fun.

"Gloria" was Susan Drury who led the rosary at church, because she got really loud when she said that part of the prayers. "*Glory* to God…"

Uncle Pete became "Hank"—he owned a Hardware Hank franchise.

"Box" was the private nickname of a girlfriend of mine, with measurements of 32–32–32.

"Toon" was Fred next door who had perfect features, deep set eyes, a pronounced nose, head set in a forward mode like he is going somewhere, and dyed black hair, and looked like the silhouette of the cartoon character Fred Flintstone.

A drug store clerk who made one word of "Haveaniceday" became "Niceday lady." Each of their cars had a nickname—"Malesia," "Spanglish," and "Buck" for the Buick that lost the *i* off the trunk's silver lettering.

They were friends like that—the ones you can't help yourself but to love.

If you knew Barry or Ceci, you were forever an important part in their life. They made you feel good whenever you encountered them—beer or no beer, I will add.

# I Hate the Word Orphaned

SEE, MOM AND DAD were gone from our lives. I was seventeen when Mom died, and just seven when Dad died in a car accident. At age seven, I was just getting old enough to recognize what a family is all about, who an aunt was, that moms and dads owned all the children, and most families had rules and allowance and about the different roles of parents, aunts, priests, and sisters in my life. I didn't get to know Dad as Dad really at all. But my mom was a very special parent; she was both Mother and Father rolled into one, but only then till I was age seventeen. Then her love, character, precious heart, care, gentleness, great intelligence, and security left me to go to Heaven. No waiting room time in Purgatory for that woman—she had an elevator ride straight up to the open pearly gate, welcome mat emblazoned with "Welcome Mrs. Sharmaine O'Brien." I'd like to believe that. Ceci recited that pine often when we talked about Mom.

My sister, Clarey, apparently inherited a good DNA sampling of Mom's glorious qualities, as everyone in our outreach family tells us. She was almost seven years older than me, and so got to know our mom longest.

Ceci—well, Ceci was about as independent and fractiously variable as they make 'em; sometimes like incarnate

28

or hatched, she was so independent. Maybe like my dad, but I don't know. Her lack of propriety in social situations floored me—a sort of accepted innocent irreverence. You would never know she had any authoritative parent, fearless to risk embarrassment, ask any question, and first most to challenge a seemingly illogical statement. Courage with conviction. She would shake a person's hand and introduce herself if they said hello to her in the bank or grocery store, even at age ten. She conducted herself like a princess tomboy. She could sing and play any musical instrument she looked at, almost like a svente. It was eerie, what a natural musical talent she was. And she could change our car's oil and can pickles. Thank goodness she wanted to be a high school teacher, working with inquisitive but know-it-all teens, because she knew *everything* or would find it out in a short while and consequently really primed the curiosity of young minds.

Clarey was the demure one—owned a quiet fervor for life, and knew from her start that God was bigger than Elvis. She apparently had been indoctrinated to the Catholic Church practices the most by our father. Tootsie said Clarey had Catholic grace and quiet intelligence.

Being the oldest of us, Clarey transparently acted as our mom, as much as we would allow. She and Aunt Tootsy (Betsy, really, who always had Tootsie Rolls on hand for us) did a wonderful job raising us. Young but smart and worldly, we three decided we totally wanted to be on our own and so took over Dallas and Sharmaine O'Brien's little house in Harrington as homeowners at extremely young ages for such. And we survived quite well, thank you. You see, God apparently predestined us orphans into financial health. I am sure that Mom and Dad had taken the acts to have mortgage insurance, auto coverage, and huge life insurance policies to keep us healthy but had no expectations (nor did Metro Life) that they would pass so early from their lives.

How we grew to be so well rounded is a mystery to me, but by God's shining graces, it happened for us, and we were growing up and adapting to our lives without parents. We survived well. Some days now, I hardly thought of missing our mother and father; we had made a new tight little secure family, the three of us.

# School's Out—Car Wreck

THE PHONE RANG, THE caller asking for Clarey O'Brien. I answered saying this was Clarey's sister. The caller identified herself as a nurse from St. Francisca Hospital where Clarey worked. I told her that my sister, Clarey, is actually there, working on third floor. "Is something wrong?"

After establishing the hierarchy of our little household family and my HPPA prerogative right to know, the voice on the other end of the line informed me that my sister Ceci was in the hospital emergency room. Her car had hit a tree. She suffered a cut on her arm requiring stitches and had some bruising. The voice informed me that a doctor was with her. "And a police officer," the voice added.

"What happened? Where is the cut? How serious? Is it deep? Is she bleeding? How bad is it? Is she conscious?" A million questions came out of me and got audibly thrown at the voice on the phone. "Where in the hospital are you? Can you get my sister Clarey down there? Was anyone with Ceci in the car?" Then it registered, "Why is there an officer there? Was someone else hurt?" I was not waiting for any answers.

Finally, when I gasped for air because my larynx was constricting in an anxious twitch, the voice was able to break in. Vomit sat in my upper G.I. "She has several scratches and a cut requiring just a few stitches. She will be fine. Clarey O'Brien? I know now why Ceci O'Brien seemed like a familiar name. I know the nurse, Clarey, your other sister. I'll page her to come down. Do you have anyone there with you? Do you drive? You may want to come to the hospital, but I will find Clarey and get her here with Ceci."

My larynx emitted and "Urhm", as I invisible to her, nodded.

She continued, "The officer is here because of a concern about the vehicle involved in the accident and of course, your sister. Do you want me to tell her you will come here to be with her too?"

I got the particulars and dialed Clarey's cell which she answered just as they paged her to report to ER ASAP. She was working second shift on the third floor, her first week of rotation in psych.

"Oh, God. I knew it!' was her first response. Normally calm and walking with the sweet serenity God gave her, Clarey reacted panicked for a minute just as I had, spewing out similar questions to my inquiries. She got to the ER hallway with her cell phone and locked her eyes on Ceci as we talked, so she could reassuringly tell me what had happened. "I see Cec sitting up. Looks okay... She is talking to a cop... Mike Dairnerd is talking to her. Oh, God. What has happened?"

Pause and another, "Urhm" came from me.

"She looks good, Margo. I'll call you right back—when I know."

In the seven minutes till the phone rang again, I stared at the computer I had been Googling on. I started to type "driving under the influence" in the Google line. And I prayed—my own words, no logic to my ritual—partials of a Hail-Mary-Our-Father-Act-of-Contrition prayers, ending with "Make her safe, Amen."

My phone buzzed. "She's fine. She's not drunk. They tested her. Mike Dairnerd said she smelled like beer, but she was not legally drunk." Clarey needed to tell me when she called back. "They checked her alcohol level. She hit a tree though. A dog darted in the street on Bedrock Road, which she swerved for; then a kid came after the dog so she kept on getting out of the way avoiding the little girl and rammed into a tree on the curb. It was really a blessing it came down this way. However, she had beer on her breath. She is not legally drunk though, Mike said," Margo repeated. "Or he is letting her off the hook again, Margo. We'll be home in an hour when I'm off shift. Ceci can lie here till I come get her. Her stitches are little. It's a tiny cut but deep from something sharp that clipped on the visor. My friend from school, Shari Barnes, the trauma nurse, is going to let her stay in ER. Don't come down. Look up how to do a disquisitive intervention. Mike mentioned it. I don't know. What do we do?"

I Googled more, anything my frazzled mind could think of, "Help for beer drinkers."

I Googled "Alcoholics Anonymous," "charges involving beer," and "family interventions."

I Googled "alcoholism intervention process and family interventions."

I Googled treatment centers plus 60933, our zip, as it asked for.

There were three. One was the O'Brien (ironic, O'Brien, our last name) Treatment Center—in-patient, foundation sponsored, and six months minimal treatment stay.

There was St. Assisi's Day Treatment, and Mount Carbul. The website was defunct. Phone number in last year's book but not this year's. Guess it went belly up—*beer belly up*, my mind wondered.

Just the two places then.

Thoughts filtering through my head went quickly about what to do. Ceci didn't have six months of her life to give up to this embarrassment. She *did* have three months—summer break.

*Oh, God. Oh, Mom, are you watching? Was Ceci really an alcoholic and were we denying it? Oh, I'm so stupid. No. Not one of Sharmaine O'Brien's children an alcoholic. We are Irish though. Gees, Ceci. You can leave it alone most of the time. I knew it. I knew it in my gut. She is alcoholic. Damn! Should I call the phone numbers before Clarey gets here? Should I get Barry over here? Do we have to do this tonight? School would be out in six days and she could possibly have until the very first of September to get her life back together to fulfill her teaching contract she signed for next fall. There goes her summer of fun.* My mind was racing like my pulse. Fun might be what got her here. I nervously clicked on "Facility Information" on one of the sites.

St. Assisi Day Treatment was out. Night time was when Ceci drank. *Isn't night time when most people drink?* I processed. Day treatment was just a silly thought somebody had. *Dumb,* I thought. *They need night treatment. Evening is when drinkers drink.*

So the O'Brien Treatment Center it was.

And we convinced a psychologist and a counselor at the O'Brien Treatment Center during the pre-evaluation assessment meeting to minimize Ceci's conviction time to three months and fifteen days. "Yes, we will treat her during her summer break." Out just in time for fall semester to start. Darn, Ceci and Barry were scheduled to learn to take flight instruction in a single engine Cirrus this summer. She won't be able to do that if she is put away. Oh, what an ugly phrase—"put away."

# *Intervention*

THAT FIRST NIGHT IN the hospital and now on intervention eve, Barry came. Barry was Ceci's "bestest" friend from playground days. They never were anything less than the best of best friends. He had seen her in little-girl underpants and no T-shirt. She had seen him naked behind the shed when she asked what a penis looked like. They had laughed and cried together often. They tried their first kisses together. They loved each other. They caught squirrels together, had a fake slap fight over which end of the canoe they got, and paddled down the river happily anyway. Barry promised to be her best man and she would be his. They jumped the same ramp simultaneously and fell off bikes together and had matching knee scars, a story they shared with each new acquaintance, telling every other line of the story in synchronization just like the bike jump. That kind of friendship.

Barry was her drinking buddy and would be most influential coming to O'Brien's Treatment Center with us on a visit. A plurality of her trusted school friends, the sister of a counselor from O'Brien's facility whom Clarey knew from nursing school, us two, and Aunt Tootsy, our since-we-were-little adopted/surrogate mom were all there. Ceci knew we were arranging this. We invited her. It wasn't

36

like the 20-20 television shows where they trick the drin-
kee into attending and shut the door with her best friends
and family and some bad-haired step-sibling sitting there
to intervene. We were going to have more of a social come-
to-Jesus conciliatory meeting, if you will. Barry started.
Hell, Barry, possibly himself alcoholic now I wonder, handled predominantly most of it. I guess who should know
why, how, or how often Ceci drank better than Barry? Ceci
was in agreement from the first sentence. She didn't like
drinking beyond good manners. She conceded that perhaps some "out of control behavior" grabbed some part of
her and often said, "Hmmm, this tastes and feels goood.
Let's have more." She knew it was out of proportion in her
life. That was easy. She owned up to that. She will stay at
the green institution for the stint offered.

Barry offered he envied her getting help. He pledged
to quit drinking all liquor and beer in her honor and in
support of her.

Our intervention went well to our surprise.

We joked about going out for drinks after the intervention. But then Clarey thought better about it, having
hot tea and icy raspberry tea since there was combination
of anxiety in the room with having the cold shakes and
sweaty nervousness. We all went home after eating last
night's pizza and off to bed content enough with the hellish decision we had had to make. All of us but Ceci, who
dreamt of going to a fiberglass green bed with a green mat-
tress and green cover in a green-walled room.

# Ceci's Treatment

WE WERE FORCED TO wait two hollowing long weeks before visiting Ceci O'Brien at O'Brien's Institute. Maybe it wouldn't be so hubristically humiliating since she was named O'Brien, my brain toyed with hopefully. Maybe people would think she was the proprietor, the daughter of the owner, or some equivalent nonsense ran through my head, wanting special treatment for my sister. No one is allowed to visit till after fourteen days, they told us. Canons, rules, always rules within an institution. So much so that they paralyze even visitors.

We walked into the day room after two weeks. That is such an oppressive sadness. The word day room itself conjures up an institutional setting—a mentally ill facility. Done in endemic army green, iron bars on high windows, dull looking and no decor, a large graffiti-covered cell. Why not call them something cute like they do at day care centers or care facility…coined acronyms or positive sounding names—activity center, the coloring room, the rec area, play station—but day room? It makes you depressed just to say it. A place where people sit for hours each day—a day room. We sat at the customary visitor side flank of the institutional military green table on sturdy unbreakable yellowed fiberglass chairs when the door to the hall of dorm rooms opened. In walked what used to be Ceci, dragging one slippered foot after the other and barely raising her chin enough to acknowledge she knew us.

"What the fuck!" screamed Clarey. Clarey never swore. "What the fuck?" she repeated again and looked at me with a quick sideways turn of the head and back, as if confirming with the rest of us that her eyes were seeing this, and it was real. She hugged a nearly unresponsive Ceci and walked right past our sister to a nursing service window in the getting-uglier-by-the-minute ugly "day room." She talked there briefly and moved into a corridor, raising her cell phone to her ear as I watched.

Ceci pad-footed her way over to our green table. I stood up not knowing whether to hug the blob that had the persona of my sister or stand there with my arms down and mouth open. It took a second to sink in. This was *really* Ceci. Oh my god!

"What are they giving her? Is she on Xanax?" I Tourette's-like asked the nurse who now attempted to assist Ceci to a sitting position in a fiberglass dull yellow chair.

"Yes." she confirmed. "She will only be like this a couple of hours. You caught her just a few minutes after her meds were given. She won't be like this by ten o'clock. She will be more like herself after that. She has a nightly dose and one in early morning. She had a little fractious situation during the d.t.'s and was striking out at staff and others, so she was prescribed a calming drug."

*D.t.'s? She never drank that much…Oh. Yeah, she did.* Reality set in around me.

Clarey had walked back in from the hall toward Cec and me and announced that Ceci would not be on Xanax tomorrow morning to the nurse standing with us. Dr. Limus had ordered it tapered down as the week progressed but said he should have done it earlier. He apologized. "Gees!" Clarey said disgustingly for all present to hear.

*What would Mom say?* I thought. Ceci striking out. Us sitting in an ugly dayroom, one of us involuntarily incarcerated. "What would Mom say" ran through me, and my body did a strange all-over shiver, while my belly jumped up into my chest wall. Ick. My face gills instantly engaged with nauseating vertigo.

Noticing our upset, Ceci said slowly but lucidly, interspersed with pauses, "It's okay. I think I kicked a nurse the other night. It was worse than I thought, quitting beer. I drank every day, you know. Well, not here of course." Her humor indelibly inflicted. There is my sister. I bent over to her and hugged her hard. Clarey got in the triangle with us and the three plastic chairs and we passed goodness among our tripodally-connected hearts.

The sixth week, Ceci came home with us on a pass from her usurped incarceration, as long as there was supervision.

"That's it then," Ceci said.

The water just ran from the kitchen faucet without Ceci even noticing. She held her cup next to the sink while the water ran down the drain. Clarey was peeling potatoes and I was answering e-mails at the kitchen computer.

"Mom was addicted. I suppose that is where I got it" was all she said while the water ran needlessly.

"Mom drank?" I asked, startled.

I knew nothing of my mother drinking. I couldn't fathom pious Mrs. O'Brien had an indiscretion. I know I was the youngest, but surely, I would have seen Mom drink—cans or bottles, arguments over it, drunken nights, something in my seventeen years with her! How could I not know my mother's privations of alcohol?

Clarey's shoulders dropped; I could see her back read-just. She rested her forearms next to the potatoes and set down the peeler. She turned so slowly a turtle would have beaten her. My head cocked unconscionably her direction, my ears like listening for a loud speaker to repeat the announcement.

"What?" Clarey finally mouthed, lips stuck together.

"Mom was obsessive compulsive, we all know that. She shopped like crazy. It was like an addiction, people say. *Psychology Today* articles say shopping can be an addiction… We grew up at the mall for Chrissakes, girls!" She threw her hands up in the air in gesturing emphasis. "You know she loved shopping. Ads were all she read of the Sunday paper. Big salty pretzels and Orange Julius were part of my diet from age four till she died."

We didn't say a word. She finally shut the water off and set down her cup, never even filling it.

"Great Uncle Sid drank a lot—on Dad's side," Clarey finally responded getting her lips apart now. "I barely knew Sid. I was little when he died. He lived in Seattle until just before Dad died so he hardly came to our house or was present in my life." What did my oldest sister have to tell me? I waited. "Mom kind of avoided him and all I remember is, he smelled. I suppose he smelled like beer if I were going to guess about my memory.

"God must be calling your name, Ceci," Clarey said. "Just listen."

# Al from Allstate

So Ceci fulfilled her stay at the O'Brien's Treatment Center, getting out just perfectly in time for the fall school semester orientation day—with recovery, as it is termed, underway. Not exactly her most exciting summer but one of the best of her summers in reality. In reality, that was how she spent this one. She continued the progressive life style with a twelve-step program, learned skills in the culinary program to bake breads, read up how to fly an airplane, and became an even better person, if that was possible. What a change in her. I noticed a spiritual lift every week or so, a shift of maturity in her thinking, like wisdom about life. She was lighter, happier, and full of gratitude. She talked about God's prodigious existence in her every moment with great applaud. Clarey and I almost wished we were alcoholic to be allowed into her Alcoholics Anonymous meetings and get that same inner beauty of mind and spirit she was gaining from the fellowship. Ah, sweet serenity. God grant me that too. It seemed Ceci carried a secret that gave her peacefulness. It was so noticeable in everything she did, mostly in her interactions with people.

While we sat around the first day Cec was home, feeling just a little awkward, wondering if we have new roles to help Ceci now that she was not drinking. She picked up a caramel apple and took a huge bite leaving a twenty-inch thread of caramel between the stick and her mouth. She maneuvered the apple up in the air and let the thread curl itself into her fish-like agape mouth, her neck all awkward as she strained to hold it directly aligned under the apple. "Guess I'll just eat, since I can't drink. Probably look like Uncle Sid too." She laughed. He was a 300-pound short man. We all just giggled, the ice broken.

We were deep into understanding why she drank, former relatives' addictions, and our genetics conversation when the doorbell rang. Ceci almost knocked her chair over at the disrupting sound, thankful for an escape, I think, from the soul-searching explanations of what had been happening in her life.

A cute nicely-dressed guy put his hand out to shake Ceci's. Caramel apple in one hand and caramel sticky goop in the other, she made an arrested hands-up gesture in return to his outstretched hand. She pointed at the apple to make sure he got it and reassumed the police-are-here position, with her arms up.

"Hi-I'm-Alvin-Stephens-with-Allstate-Insurance-did-you-know-you-are-on-a-flood-plain-with-all-the-rain-this-last-spring-I-am-sure-you-have-thought-about-that. I can make sure you never lose the value of your home assets. Oh-are-you-the-home-owner? Is-uh-your-mom-home?" he said all in one breath. Ceci was petite and really did look young.

Ceci slammed the door shut—only to open it immediately. His face was that of an eleven-year-old Alvin when his dad took only his brother fishing and left Alvin all disappointed at home. "Just kidding," she said when Ceci reopened the door. "I always wanted to do that, and they are pestering me in here. My mom's…and you are an insurance sales agent…never mind. Yeah, um, we are worried about flooding. I'm building an ark for the flood out back. Do you want to see it?"

Alvin from Allstate just stood there skeptically, with his jaw all funny, bottom lip out, mouth agape now. He had never in all his two-months with the company had anybody slam a door in his face or joke with him.

"Do you, Al from Allstate? Want to see the ark?"

That was her kind of humor—off the wall, catch you off guard, and always make you smile at ease.

Al came in just like that to become another friend of Ceci's. She bought Al's flood insurance, just to make him feel good, I swear. We knew, after that fun encounter, that we had our Ceci back in psychologic balance. "Al from Allstate" became his nickname. Sometimes we called him "A.A." for short.

Cec fell right back into routines with school and most of her friends. She drank soda when she went out socially, and amazingly never succumbed again to her alcohol addiction. This AA thing really worked, to the effect that she influenced others to attend meetings with her.

She handled the after treatment better than any other treated people we knew—no setbacks. Eventually, she was strong enough to attend parties and restaurants where folks drank, but she herself never held anything stronger than soda. She rarely hung out at O'Malley's with her friends. I am sure that was difficult. But she learned that she could hold a mug with soda in it and nurse it a whole evening. She learned to trick insistent friends by dumping drinks out or leave unopened bottles behind something. The bartenders knew to pour her a ginger ale in a mug, so folks would quit asking. She was amazing with her inner strength. She gave all the credit to God, her AA program, and its people. We noticed she never minded not having the beer. Whatever had gotten her into the alcoholic situation? Did it start right after dad died? We never questioned her—our—miracle. If you have alcoholism in your family, you have alcoholism in your family. Clarey and I decided not to test if we had the DNA and gave up our wine and margaritas right when Cec did.

# Northern Lights

## Pay Attention to This Moment, and the Next, and...

WE TOOK OFF ON Labor Day weekend to a little resort along Lake Michigan, near Duluth—just to reset our juices and be together without our other demands of life. The first morning, there was a slight fog out on the lake, and the ships were bellowing to each other. We listened to the soft interrupted silence as we sipped our coffee on the flatter stones along the rocky shore by our cabin. Wow, such serenity and security among us and God. Ceci's new ideals were rubbing off on us as she mentored her progressive and positive new spirituality—another gift of the AA promises.

We rock-climbed, shopped the gift shops, trekked up the lighthouse stairs, hiked to a picnic spot, climbed through streams, and took photographs like crazy to capture the autumn beauty and peacefulness forever. We did a little gambling too in the casinos along the route into Canada.

Later that evening, Clarey had caught the northern lights presenting themselves as she took the trash out from the cabin and yelled for us to come see them. We got neck strain standing and watching after half an hour or so and eventually just laid on the resort driveway, flat on our backs, heads together, like spokes with a hub.

"That's what I picture heaven is like," I told the gals as we lay on the broken asphalt, like membranes of a sideways slice of lime watching rainbows unfold and bleeding tails of colors.

"I think heaven is every second more exciting than the last and you are so happy with anticipation, you just nearly itch for the next flood of beauty and wonder to come over you, complete peace with nothing else to do, like watching northern lights," I said. "God is there to talk with and calm us and it's all white and angel web like. You get to see everyone you have ever known with their faces content and bodies dancing, flitting, touching, hand-holding like a square dance promenade with everyone else. It's better than any feeling ever we have known—not an orgasm, not a whirring merry-go-round ride, not being held tight by our mother's arms, but better than that," I added. "What do you think is heaven?"

Ceci agreed that her picture of heaven was similar— neon northern lights but the whole of heaven was being held in this surreal pastel painting of Jesus's arms. Clarey had a shelving effect with hell, purgatory, and inhabitation of heaven making up the shelves of cloud layers, she said, with better lighting, air quality, and serenity as you rose up the levels. So goes for our Catholic upbringing and interpretations. Mostly from some ancient artist's depiction.

I wondered if I had continued with the aspirant to be a candidate to be a novice to be a nun application, if I would know more about what the kingdom of heaven would have to offer. I would imagine those same pictures were used in nun school.

We talked all night. We had the conversation—a morbid but necessary conversation. The heaven talk kind of set the pace.

I asked, "Hey, what would you guys put on my tombstone?" After much discussion, we determined that Clarey's monument would read "Full of Grace," and Ceci's would be "Remarkable," and I, the youngest of course, they said, would be "To Be Determined." They said, like in my current real estate apprenticeship, I'm not old enough to have a legacy! Ceci said that I had not earned my wings yet.

Talk about dying with honor. I wasn't old enough.

# And Then It Happened

SURPRISE. PERIOD, NOT AN exclamation mark.

I sat there for a long time.

When we heard that Ceci had a cancer, we expected she would fly through the treatment, just like she did alcohol treatment and come out smelling like a rose. So much for expectations.

None of what happened with her cancer story smelled like a rose, not even the thousands of roses Barry and her friends sent to her. Or the decades of novenas I made.

I sat there for a long time. Clarey was playing the piano, and Cec was editing music sheets for the guitarist at St. Mary's the Sunday two months after visiting Duluth. She misspoke, or so we thought. "I need to put the toothpicks up on the stripes. Where is the underwood?" she said. We all smiled. In the next minute, Ceci smiled and laughing, saying, "What just came out of my mouth!" as if she retrieved her own cacophony from the air. And she stood there, more astonished than either of us.

There were more indications, but we ignored them. Ceci was always making fun. She was always coining words or phrases, and we thought she was being silly. She had asked us to pass the shoes and socks, meaning salt and pepper at lunch.

She missed a dinner date with a friend she loves last week, forgetting their plans. It was the Our Lady of Fat-Em-Up Club, first Tuesday of the month dinner-with-dessert outing, which had been happening for a couple of years. We all thought she just didn't realize it was a new month or a Tuesday, or some silly memory tic. She just failed to go.

# It Just Doesn't Make Any Sense

"IT JUST DOESN'T MAKE any sense." These are the words to this day that I can't speak.

Ceci called me while I was out for breakfast with a friend. "What Cec? Is that you?" I said, listening to a soft voice that sounded once removed.

"It just doesn't make any sense. I wanted to go to school, but I am afraid I won't find my way home. I just got up and had an automobile for breakfast, but I can't make any sense of it. The school moved across the street."

She was dead serious. It was unbelievable to hear her voice saying weird concoctions.

Without paying at the restaurant, I grabbed my purse and jumped in the car. In the seven-minute trip, I shivered, wondering if I should have called an ambulance. What would I find at home? Did she have a breakdown? Did she wake up and drink? It's the first day of school. What? Should I call Clarey? She is in Egypt. Okay, so I reviewed in my mind what I knew. Ceci found my number on her cell, she knew it was morning, her voice was clear; she was cognizant that her own thinking was not right. She was dying? Stroking? Or was she drinking?

Last month, just before her birthday, she called me at work with a similar fright in her voice. "Margo, there is something wrong. I can't make sense of it. My words won't come." We spent forty-eight hellish hours with doctors and evasive tests and monitors observing Ceci, with Clarey and I sitting up watching her through the night. But she had been fine since then. Well, till now. "Concussion, maybe," the doc told us then.

Why did God put Clarey in the nursing exchange program in Egypt right now? We need her. We need her leg of the tripod. *I* need her leg of the tripod.

*****

The Next Day

Ceci's Diary                    August 21

We read later an entry of that same day:

> *Barry called that there were coming and she stayed overnight. Said I didn't make sense tonight. Must be tierd. I worry that I am crazy. I was okay by my standards.*

"It's possibly an aneurysm or a stroke," the doctor said now.

"What?" we three said in unison, Barry there for the brunt. She's twenty-nine!

Then came the diagrams. "This is your brain. This is your blood normally. This is what we think is happening in your head right now," the doctor said as he sketched rough drawings and showed us x-rays on a monitor. The explanation was that a vessel in Ceci's head had a slight block-age passing through, perhaps had passed through earlier and left detectable swelling and damage. We were not sure how much damage and would not know for forty-eight hours, he continued. She may have been passing these clots for months without cognitive issue. Usually the first for-ty-eight hours after a stroke are the most important to diag-nose what is happening or what actually has happened, and of course, indicate if full recovery is possible.

"You can see in your sister the confusion, walking as if off balance and having no sense of "Ischemic or hem-orrhagic stroke most likely," the physician went on. "We call them trans ischemic attacks, but there is no apparent cascading paralysis."

Ceci was not hospitalized, but every minute in the next forty-eight was very tenuous and a constant repeti-tion from all of us: "It just doesn't make any sense." What else could we say? Ceci always made sense, even when she teased and joked. She always spelled it out, never leaving anyone not understanding her kind humor. Clever witted, she was always making acronyms out of the conversation topic. Sometimes she was so funny trying to come up with words to fit her acronymic topic, she rambled nonsensical. We hadn't noticed her illness.

She broke the ice after forty-nine hours. "Halo. I'm back." She smiled. "I saw Jesus. He has a scar on his palm like yours from the pen prick, Margo." She teased. But we weren't reassured she was back.

# The Cell Phone

WHEN CECI ENTERED THE clinic that December afternoon, she left her cell phone in the clinic's waiting room chair. That was when I knew. That was the real indication and my moment of realization that this was real bad. Ceci never left her cell phone. This one incredulous moment flooded me with reality. It was always on her person, on a rook's hook, usually with her finger in it. She did worry about someone stealing it. She kept everything on there...calendar, dates, addresses, pictures. She would give me the cell to hold only on rare occasions when physical need required relinquishment, occasions like peeing. That December afternoon, there it lay unattended on the green vinyl waiting room chair.

"I'll bring your phone, Cec," I said to her back as she headed down the hall to the exam room. No response. Then I knew. She didn't care about her phone. Something was really wrong.

"My first diagnostic observations emphasize the conclusion that further prognostic indicators must be compiled. I see similar symptoms to your August event but cannot confirm without further diagnostics and evaluative measures," the internist told us in the green clinic room.

"We're going to the hospital, Ceci," I explained to Ceci as we left the clinic building. Her eyes were hollow—round gels of pretty color, with absolutely no cognizance of me—glossy emptiness behind them, like floating irises. I led her across the hospital parking lot just yards from the clinic door.

"Well I guess I am going crazy. I can't make any sense. They might have to put me in an institution. I hate green," she told Barry. It all made sense, but it didn't. Barry just stared, socks knocked right off.

Of course she hates green. Her previous treatment center was covered with green on the walls, the chairs, and floor. It's a good thing that I was so close to Ceci. I now would have to interpret her words and phrases for others. The reference to the green theme about an institution made total sense to me—but *not* to anyone else hearing her. It was the beginning of a long horrible psychological ride for me. I didn't know it yet.

That afternoon, my fun loving of a sweet woman, intelligent, talented sister sat in her hospital bed rocking, anxiety ridden with thought disruption causing her to constantly go back and forth with her torso. The nurse stopped in to tell her nefariously she needed to lie calmly. "You will need to remain sedated as another aneurysm or trans ischemic attack could recur. You are NPO until diagnostics and lab levels are determined."

"Cec. Try to stay still," I restated more simply for the nurse, my hand calmingly on her shoulder. *Don't give her technical lingo. She thinks she's crazy, Goddammit. Be kind*, I thought.

*Where is Clarey?* I cried inside, as Barry said it out loud. With all her medical knowledge, I knew Clarey could offer better comforting words and help quell Ceci's anxiety. Ceci is too wonderful. We shouldn't have to know about this stuff.

*Goddammit,* I said to myself again. *We lost our parents. Where is the sense in this? Oh my god. I am saying it again.* "It just doesn't make any sense."

The next morning, test after test after slated test. Probes, needles, hook ups, strange machines, goo on her forehead, strange noises, tunneled x-rays, strange lights, give blood, pee in a cowboy hat, give more blood, and lie still.

I called Clarey in Egypt. She began with all sorts of parlous questions. "Hold on, Clarey. Let me tell you what I know and then you can help me form the right questions to talk to the doctor," I interrupted her. "Ceci is just a little off kilter. She makes sense part of the time. They think it is…" And I filled her in on all I knew. Clarey was silent on the other end of the line. No more questions. I thought the phone connection had broken.

"Clar?" I said.

"Yeah, Margo. I'm here…" She broke into convulsive sobbing, I could hear. "…I need to be there though." More silence except for big sobbing sniffs.

"Feel my love through my voice, hon," I said to her. "Barry is helping me…us. The docs and nurses are really good and attentive. Your nursing friends, Shar and Dennis, have been in to check on us every other hour."

"Good," finally came across a million miles. "You've done all the right stuff, sis," the voice far in Egypt affirmed.

"I'll get home as soon as I can. Have Shar call me at this number right away. Tell her docs to call me. Tell them about me being in Cairo and–and it's hard to call and catch you guys. Tell them to…oh, I don't know what. What are we going to do? What is Ceci doing now? Can I talk to her? Can she hear? Can she hear? (Her voice cracked as she repeated it.) Could she hear me if you gave her the phone?"

"Hold on," I said, and I held the receiver to Ceci's ear. Her cat's eye marble eye sockets gave me no recognition. "It's Clarey—in Egypt," I said.

Her lips started to form "What?" but nothing came.

"Talk to her Clarey…" I whispered leaning toward the voice mic. A minute later, maybe, I removed the phone from Ceci's verklempt ear, like I was sucking a frog up from the dirt. It was stuck to Ceci's clammy cheek, and there was no movement except the cord. Ceci lay like she had before the call. No excitement. No cognizance. No life.

Oh my god.

*Dear St. Jude, faithful friend of Jesus, patron saint of the hopeless, of things despaired, Pray for Cec. Come to my assistance in this great need that I may receive the help of heaven in all necessities and sufferings.*

Ceci rallied a bit hours later. She said she felt like a cushion of pins by nightfall. A cushion of pins—she'd coined another phrase. She asked Barry if he could see light through her. She laughed. We slept in the institutional green chairs—well, slept a bit anyway.

# "It Just Doesn't Make Any Sense" Again and Again and Again

THE WHOLE STORY, HUH?

Ever been in the position to decide if they pull the tubes on an already-been-labeled-dying person?

I'll espouse a bit about my part in Ceci's dying. That's all I know. I can't know her feelings and thoughts. I will share the tale of living as the living while the dying die: from the earliest development of their illness to the days just after death—not from the dying person's perspective—but from those they leave behind.

I can only best depict the living person's experiences, not the dying—from why I would get to stay upright on the earth's soil? The feelings, the despair, the smashed dreams, the experiences of becoming responsible for a sister who had nurtured you from childhood, and of walking someone to their death. I share all—the scares, the mistakes, the anxiety, the pulling away, family secrets, health issues, and values toward eventual death. Being grown up with your siblings is examined in ways that few people can verbalize. Letting go of someone you love is the bottom of the bottom of the pits.

Problems in our health care system are everywhere when you are a depressed living sibling watching someone die in a hospital. The adage of "joys shared are multiplied and sadness shared is divided" is so exemplified while riding the tribulations, searching for some hope, some joy that might be left before death occurs.

Diagnosis of cancer made by a physician began with questions about symptoms, followed by an exam looking for physical signs of a tumor. A tumor pressing anywhere along the nerve swells the area, causing a condition called papilledema. Muscle function, reflexes, and the ability to feel pin pricks in certain areas are affected. We had started with those tests in the clinic and continued in the hospital, again on Day Two.

A number of specific examinations detected Ceci's tumors: Computerized Axial Tomography, Electroencephalography (EEG), x-ray of the skull, and the Echoencephalography (EEC).

Cec said that was a lot of *E*'s after being told what tests were ahead. But she was so tired looking. She laid flat out, no energy, her eyeballs still gel-covered colored marbles. Some thinking was going on in there, but mostly we saw a visual expression of confusion.

All these tests were painless.

The real pain here is indescribable…fear of the unknown. That was the pain I was having. And probably Ceci. But she couldn't say that; she just looked scared. My vibrant, loving, lovable, perfect sister was lying in a white-sheeted hospital bed, she nearly the same color and silent and still.

An immediate biopsy and removal surgery was undeniably ordered.

I dialed Clarey every three or four hours. She was en route home and available only in strategic cell locations. "What a shittin-shituation," Barry said Ceci would say, if she could.

There's a side to the diagnosis that isn't about surgery or drugs or radiation. Our bodies and minds are not separate. A diagnosis of cancer is a powerful stimulus on the mind and emotions. Relatives and friends also have to discover how to cope with it. The victim—oh my god, Cec is a *victim*—has to adjust to dying with these people instead of living with these people. We all bear great emotional burdens and must build mutual understanding and trust in this now-different phase of our life and their death time.

# Glio-Um-Ah-Um-Ah-Blast-Huma-Huh?

GLIOBLASTOMA MULTIFORMAE. PHONETICALLY EASY. That is what it is called. I repeated it for Clarey. We sat motionless in the outer perimeters of a Surgery Family Waiting Room. No one had to say the real question on our minds. The doctor spoke to us. Ten close friends of Cec and us sat there. They were each her best friend, each an extension of love from and to her.

"I would say your sister has approximately three months to live. Sometimes we see a patient live up to a year with this condition, but due to the placement of the tumor, grading, and paucity, we would guess in your sister's case, a three to three-and-a-half-month length of time. If no post op complications occur, there may be a time of quality life for her within that period."

Whoooah. Hold the phone. You are not talking about *my* sister, are you?

If there was any small wonder in all of this period, there was one on the day of surgery. Clarey's favorite friend at the hospital just happened to be the best brain surgeon west of the Mississippi. Dr. Carlson had been on vacation, but this wonderful man, Clarey's friend, in the middle of his Christmas vacation decided to give up his family time for Ceci's surgery. He was a blessing among the hell we were sitting in.

My prayers are always words of thanks and praise. I try not to pray for things I *want* in life or ask for help all the time. After all, I have the superficial everything I need. Wants are just stuff. I figured if I prayed with worship and adoration, there wouldn't be any need to ask for things and there wouldn't be any need to beg for things. I felt short-changed. I had prayed for the right reasons, but God still did not dish out perfection for my life. Right now, he was giving me and my sisters Hell on Earth.

We then had more Hell days every day. I wondered if I had entered the convent, if God would have been better to us, if he would have not given us this horribleness to endure. I immediately thought of the semen lying on the black pleat that kept me from becoming a Sister to God.

"The bad news is Ceci has a brain tumor. It is not known as cancer. But it is in every aspect of the word. We see no varietal groupings, rather finger-like adhesions." It took approximately 45 minutes to tell us what all took place in the surgical theatre and answer our questions. Every word the surgeon said hung in the air. This was not what we were wanting to hear. A conundrum occurred. How can our ears hear the voice, process them through our intellect, and our hearts not accept the meaning of the words? It just doesn't make any sense. Ceci was all bubbles last Christmas. She gave Clarey and I green fiberglass furniture from O'Brien's Treatment Center's garage sale, just before we opened her real gift—new patio furniture hidden in the garage. She bought new luggage for Clarey with sand-proof wheels for Egypt. This was a girl, not a 101-year-old frail, disabled person. A girl with lots more LAs to experience, songs to come from her heart, thousands of children's lives to help form. There was "fun to be had," as Ceci often said on her way out the door to life.

Life. Now there's a word…it will soon end for her. She is going out the door on her way to death. Uck!

"It's Grade III, possibly Grade IV, with IV being the worst. If she is real lucky, she could live twelve months. Patients with this diagnosis usually live three months, maybe four," he repeated for us. My mouth suddenly couldn't speak—dry and agape, I discovered.

"Grade I and II tumors are considered 'low grade,' III and IV are 'high grade'. Seven percent of the voluminous childhood brain tumors are glioblastomas."

*I don't want to know this.*

He only said, "The bad news is…" Can you do that? Can you say on top of all the previous statements, "The *bad* news is…"?

*I don't want to be here. Load my limp body in a grocery cart and push me through this incursion. I don't want to face it or listen to any more yuck. This is not my life. This is not my sister. She is happy. She is wonderful. She makes my life what it is. She makes me happy. No, no, no, no… News, news…what an oxymoron. God? God, are you there? What the hell?*

# Stomach-Turning Sick Moment

BARRY LOOKED AT ME, then at Clarey, then at the doctor. I looked at Clarey, then at Barry. Where is our third leg of the tripod? Where is the person that is part of us? She is in another room becoming a post-surgical zombie, and I say that in the kindest sense of the word. Ceci was zombie-ing out of life with this brain tumor and the surgical interference in her body. She was not the leg in our tripod— she was a heavy load on top and one side was tipping over. *Help, somebody help. This is not real. I am not here. This is impossible. It just doesn't make any sense.*

We palled to the wall color as a group, unaware of the room or time of day. We remained there inertly till the automatic doors to the surgical corridor sounded a soft bell and Ceci's doctor disappeared into them.

I remember Ceci saying when school got out last May that she was more worn out at the end of school than any other year before. She had headaches this summer, never before. She started on a vitamin pack. Barry called the vitamins she took, her "Bartender Tom's Replacement."

*Bartender Tom's Replacement. Now, that was funny.* I smiled.

*Where am I? Help!*

"Glioblastoma is a rapidly spreading voracious tumor. The tentacles of the tumor cells grow into the surrounding tissues in the cerebral hemisphere. It may grow into the blood supply of the brain or into the cerebrospinal fluid and into the spinal cord," I read from my almost illegible notes.

A headache. Just recurring headaches, we thought. Her first symptoms were due to increased intracranial pressure resulting in an inability of the skull bones to expand. A headache, usually worse in the morning. Usually vomiting accompanies them. She had called me with terror in her voice and confusion in her words both times at 7:16 in the morning. Subtle personality changes may be noted. Language interpretation disturbances may occur. Review of Ceci's diary months later revealed she had many, many days of just not feeling well. She had cancelled her trip to visit Clarey in Egypt because of wondering if she could fly without vomiting, she later revealed, rather than her cover story about early school commitments.

Her diary entry stated: *It just doesn't make any sense why I feel this way. I am taking more vitamins and not drinking. Why am I sick?*

Left front for Cec. Most commonly, glioblastomas are in the frontal, temporal, and parietal lobes. As it grows, pressure may cause effects to distant parts of the brain. Brain resection or lobectomy may be necessary. *Don't talk about those in the same paragraph with my sister's name, please! She is a human being, not a cadaver in a medical facility's cold storage. Oh my god. Cadaver. Oooh. That is what she will be someday soon. Oh my god. I hurt. I hurt inside. I hurt in my head. I hurt in my heart. My stomach was revolting saliva.*

*Where is Ceci's mind? How is she hurting? I had a sudden urge to break into the recovery room. I did not want to miss a minute of the three or four months the surgeon promised. He did promise, didn't he? No, he didn't. It was only a maybe.*

# Won't Be Independent Again

OKAY, SO CECI HAD been the most active of us O'Brien sisters. She and Barry tried every sport known to man—rappelling, bungie-ing, hot air ballooning, marathoning, and visiting the Olympic pretrials. Her adventures filled our dinner talk loquaciously. Sometimes I wanted her life, which seemed so much fuller than mine. I could feel her zest for life when she spoke and gained enthusiasm and motivation for new experiences from just listening. She was my mentor, my mother, my leader, my teacher, my love—my sister. She told me I was all of that to her and that I inspired her. We were buckets of mushy love, us three. We were related and mushy didn't matter. It didn't matter if people had to wait for us—we threw in a tripod hug often and when we wanted to. That was…before now, before one leg was up.

Of the many words that I jotted down after talking with the surgeon, this was a phrase that stuck out in my mind and on the paper…"won't be independent again." And he felt sure that there were microscopic feelers engorging on Ceci's brain.

The doctor said some hopeful things to us, but we did not hear them. I reviewed my notes after Ceci's death and discovered that he said some—in his words, not mine—"hopeful" things. Conservative lies. End of life communication. Bet he was taught that technique in med school—probably had a whole semester on it. We didn't even hear his dichotomic efforts.

"No infarction during surgery."

"Speech should come back quickly…for the time being."

"Maybe out of the hospital in a week."

"Prognosis is three to five years…in some cases."

"Didn't have to touch or inspect the rest of the brain."

"Fairly encapsulated tumor was removed."

These were what he called hopeful things? Pre-taught intern babble.

This is not the lady in the next bed. This is not the other family in the day room. These are not research statements from a thesis. The words in the air in this room are about my family, my sister. Ceci.

It's Ceci, dammit. My sis. Zombied out and only getting worse.

# Worst Case Scenario

THE TERM WORST CASE scenario. Those words were echoed by Dr. Eastern the next day. The words wafted over my head as if I were in trance. There was little optimism in their voices as they gave the best case scenario.

The best case scenario was that the tumor would not come back, and Ceci would have one or two years of quality life. Huh. Now there is another term that stinks. While that portion of med school is great, please, I don't want to be the person that has to hear what the doctor learned to temper piss-poor news to the family after surgical invasion.

There is no best case scenario. We know it. We are in it. We are headed straight into hell. Together.

In retrospect after her death, I could see that Ceci had lived, really lived her life. Out there on the edge, in the fast lane, experiencing so much in her short twenty-nine years. God had designs only He knew about.

*Losing someone we love*
*is never easy to accept*
*especially when it happens*
*unexpectedly*

JEAN POSUSTA

*we find ourselves*
*searching for a reason*
*for what happened*
*and struggling to make*
*some sense of it all*
                    —Bessie Anderson Stanley

# Dedication Moment to Ceci

S/HE HAS ACHIEVED SUCCESS who has lived well, laughed often, and loved much; who has gained respect of intelligent men, and the love of little children; who has filled his niche; accomplished his task; who has left the world better than he found it whether by an improved poppy, a perfect poem, or a rescued soul; who has always looked for the best in others and given the best he had; whose life was an inspiration; whose memory a benediction.

Anonymous

# I'm Outta Here

CECI WALKED MORE LAPS around the hospital corridors than any other patient ever had; we had to take shifts to continue making walking rounds with her. And eventually, three days post-op that anxiety convinced a doctor that she was well enough physically to be released from the hospital as she threatened to call the cops on the nurses who would not let her out of there. She had her things packed the second night after her major brain surgery. When she did get home, she slept, only from exhaustion of those walks, and then she again became impossible to handle in her trying to escape. She wanted to walk down the stairs when she couldn't even stand alone. She got lost when led from room to room in our house. She lashed out at people. Anxiety does strange things. Near-death is not a state of living. It is a state of unreality and don't try to talk reality to those in that state. She cut her hair. She fell down walking. She fell in the bathroom. Her anxiety was so strong; her body moved but didn't perform as it should. Her anxiety was so strong; she was in the snow invincibly sans coat, shoes or assistance when anxiety kicked in. She was out in the snow.

Ceci insisted on her release from the Methodist Hospital. Her speech and strength came back a little more each day. Word-finding had been 20 percent affected pre-op and similarly, post-op.

A statistic—20 percent—had been applied to my formerly sane sister's speech capability. Gees.

Three weeks postoperative, Ceci was calmer, weaker, resting a lot, and a little coherent, much of the apparent normalcy due to liver-killing medication. However mumble-mouthed she appeared, her words were understood enough so that we could see to her needs. There was never another best case scenario moment for Ceci. She had had the best of her life before. She had had her quality of life before. And my quality of life was forever changed.

In reflection now, I suppose God did know and He did give us a warning of what was to come. He did give us some time with Ceci before death took her away from this life, but I still don't quite know how I feel about God in all of this taking someone from my life dying stuff. He did take her from us slowly, preparing us all for the outcome of this illness. He gave us a sudden warning, followed by those three to four months to prepare for the outcome. (Shiver.)

Ceci was inundated with cards of love and concern and a car full of floating Mylar, pale and feeble. Clarey decided to stay on sabbatical from her hospital work and tend to Ceci till she couldn't handle her on her own. Her speech and strength came back a little more for a while. The eyes remained mostly gel like and unrecognizable. Someone else's. Was God in there? Was He walking with her? Was her body just left here temporarily for us to get used to the idea of losing her? Her brain had left. Her communication had left. Her cognition had left. We had the shell, the worsening shell. I can only hope that God did that, that He took her soul earlier and left a bodily shell in appearance to suffer, unfeeling. I some days wanted to believe that He took her soul and mind and heart straight up with Him already. Is that possible?

Barry was her stern and helm. He knew her intrinsi-cally. In countless ways, he gave her teases and tenderness. He brought her flowers to smell, repeating their name. and reteaching her about smell. He talked with her as if she were flying a kite or riding the rollercoaster along beside him. "No grief till she leaves us." He practiced. He talked of future, he talked of past, he coined phrases about her illness. He was unbelievable. He smiled at her every time he thought she was looking…mostly through his tears.

God needs to know that Ceci is a woman who can't die. We need her. We all love her too much. Give her back. Give her back!

"What's that under the refrigerator magnet?" I nearly screamed with my horror.

# What's That Under the Refrigerator Magnet?

I WALKED INTO THE kitchen. In large script in Ceci's handwriting, there it was: *Cancer.*

*Why is this hanging here?* I wondered.

"Your sister keeps forgetting what she has. She finally wrote it down and hung it here so she wouldn't forget," my sister Clarey told me.

God. Please don't make this reminder so constantly obvious for us.

"Cornucopia," Ceci said. "I have a cornucopia," she told her friend when they stopped to see her.

At least I got to see her handwriting again.

One of the worst aspects of all this is coming to grips...coming to grips with disease and coming to grips with death. Realization is the keyword here. Your reality as you knew is no longer. You are in a Near-Death Stage of Living, which is not living. All Ceci wanted to do was escape. Escape from the hospitals, escape from the Hospice nursing home, escape from the doctor's offices, escape from the CT scan bed, escape from the MRI. Even when she got to her bedroom in her home, she couldn't escape. Her anxiety level was far beyond imaginable. We dealt with her postoperative confusion, her understanding-this-hor-rible-disease anxiety, the realization, and escape techniques associated with the C-word, fright of death, fright of real physical changes, fright of the coming bodily changes, fright of others not understanding what she was saying, fright of others not helping you, and loss of physical and mental function. All that in a perfectly normal person. It just doesn't make any sense.

# To Nuke or Not to Nuke

WE ALL KNEW. CECI did not want life support systems. She did not want chemotherapy. She did not want radiation therapy. Her doctor suggested no chemotherapy, rather a more quality living her last weeks. Ceci did not want to live with the disease, but knowing treatment would hurt her more, said no. She wanted to die when our father died and not live without him. Not that she was depressed or anything at that time, just expressing how tough it is to be the one to go on living when a major player in your life passes on. And how tough it is to have parts of your body deteriorate and not be able to do anything about it. Ceci wanted no curative measure taken should she develop a major illness. She told us years ago that life is tiring, and when it is time, just let her light go out as God suggests.

In the days between awakening with slight confusion and surgery, Ceci had signed six copies of living wills, each time a new form more legal than the last was developed. She definitely did not want to linger on machines or in a dying state. She had signed an advanced directive long ago. We did it together.

But we all continued to hold some hope. We wanted Ceci to say instead, "I want to live longer. I want to try further therapy." It was *our* only hope that Ceci could stay on the earth longer with *us*. It was about us. Each week, we would broach the question to her in a different way, hoping to trick her into changing her mind and try to convince her to have radiation or chemotherapy. "If you don't want to do it for you, Ceci, do it for me," we would selfishly plea.

We thought Ceci just might one day opt for further therapy. Her decision had been final before her surgery when she was of solid mind. Her decision was signed on paper in black and white.

Each week, I personally prodded her though, just to be on the sure side, would she now consider another form of therapy to help stop the cancer. All doctors advised against any further invasive therapy. Ceci said she would like a pill to fix this, but definitely always told us "No" to chemotherapy and radiation. In her confused ways later, she would write, "Isn't there any capsule I could take to pure my health?"

Radiation burns? Chemotherapy stints? Mexico? In the Days of Deciding where to have further anticancer treatments such as chemo or radiation, there were many family meetings and mini-meetings with Clare's professional friends. We all wanted our sister to live forever. People were talking to us about "quality of life." *We* now had to weigh the additional suffering for *her* that comes most likely with further treatments. (That's not just "possibly" or "maybe" or "never" or "occasionally" that's most likely.) Ceci would suffer again and more and have skin burning and peeling and hair loss again, vomiting, nausea, numerous trips to exhaust her—all the wonders of chemo.

In previous times, Ceci had talked with friends about their personal struggles with chemotherapy. She knew of stories. She had told me how dehumanizing and debasing it seems, as it shreds a victim's dignity to pitiful tatters, their spirits to abject poverty. We each decided in our hearts, if Cec grew well enough with strength enough to fight each of those little vomitous battles, those exhausting trips, physical battles, etc., we would really push her to have the nuke stuff. But in the overall picture, the decision was Ceci's, or rather the decision was Ceci's disease, and of course, God, who has control of it all. Without ever asking a question about the side effects, she insisted that we not take measures to possibly prolong her life with further anticancer treatments. She did not want to live in that manner. She decided that when she was eighteen, put it in writing, and had reminded each of us that many times.

"But there is always that hope of cure," her friend told her.

"Why aren't your sisters seeing to this for you?" another friend said.

"I know a case where…" More friends.

The Want-To-Do-Gooders in Life know not what they do. Ceci heard the stories over and over of helpful chemotherapy (not radiation) as we sat with her and her visitors, and she tried to process each bit of information as we did.

"Did they have brain cancer?" she would ask.

Dead end.

From the Dying Person's Bill of Rights: "I have the right to not be judged for my decisions which may be contrary to beliefs of others."

Truth be told, we would have done anything—anything—to have her forever. But God had made a decision.

# The Haircut

DURING HER TEN DAYS at home, post-op but pre-Hospice home, there were many trials.

"Oh, your hair is cut, Ceci," I said as I walked into the house when my sister was "sitting" with Cec.

Clarey explained that "Yes, Ceci's hair was cut," but "No, Clarey had not done it."

Ceci had found scissors in the bathroom and cut her hair herself. This was only an omen of more to come, little did we know. Her hair cut was what I would call globular. She had grabbed locks here and there and trimmed or just cut away. The cut had to be repaired to make her not look crazy. Ceci had occasionally cut her own hair in the Pre-Surgery Days and done it quite decently. But this—this was a torturous cut. We were lucky she did not cut her ears or her face badly considering her limited digital and functioning capabilities that week. A blessing, her regular hairdresser said nothing but positive side comments as she corrected the asymmetrical buzz.

Another concern that same week was finding Ceci at the top of our rickety wooden cellar stairs. She was not seeing well or balancing. Slight vertigo maybe? She leaned along the wall or was assisted to walk anywhere these days. She would have fallen down those steps, there is no doubt, if Clarey had not been wide awake watching what Ceci was doing up in the middle of the night.

"I'll call someone. I'll call other doctors. I'll call Hospice. I'll call the cancer center. I'll call nursing services. I call cancer units. I'll visit the chemotherapy unit with Ceci," Barry offered, when we got him away from her room, contravening her written wishes.

He did all that. We did all that. You can't escape. No matter whom you call.

Everywhere we turned for help offered more phone numbers and little help. We played telephone tag. It was non-substantiative banter.

We called everyone who in any way could offer our sister any assistance through all this. Thank God for the patience of people and those who knew we needed listening ears. There were really few favors to be had out there. Out of all the phone calls came a lot of sympathy but little toward our needs...our need to escape this terrible C-thing happening to Cec.

All calls reached a dead end.

Not a funny quip, people.

"Cornucopia," Barry said, "Yes, Cec. We have one hell of a cornucopia here."

She had spent most of the day in a rocking chair. Her feet kicked commensurate with hiking Kilimanjaro. We got a rocking chair for her care facility room to keep her from trying to walk. She had unsteady movement and stilt-like walking. Her body was succumbing to being bedfast. Cells were changing. Ugliness of dying was replacing my sister's beauty.

Barry called it speed rocking, what she would do. Her anxiety took her to unbelievable levels of driven madness like rocking. That new rocking chair wood actually split three times from her demands on its wood. We repaired and repaired.

Then she asked for a "paper of note and stencil". Barry gave it to her. She wrote out the word cancer and motioned for Barry to put it on the refrigerator.

*Great. Put a billboard up. I can't think about anything else, anyway.*

# That's for Old People

"Ceci, we are going to have to move you to a Hospice home."

Can you believe those words have to be said to someone you love in life? We all hope we never have to say that to a parent, to a person who has devoted years of their life taking care and teaching others. Societies' morals apparently have gone sideways here. Where were my morals! Take a loved one to a Hospice home? Should one of us quit our jobs to stay with our Ceci full-time instead of Hospice? Probably Clarey because of her nursing. Of course, we all want to, but want to and feasibility were different. We could not have done it—she needed full-time supervision. We could not go without sleep, and she seemed to have the stamina of a hyperactive three-year-old on steroids. In fact, she was on steroids. She could be up all night some nights. Emphasis on: we could not meet her needs. We could not provide her the round-the-clock nursing care which she now required. A Hospice home was the answer. Oh, what a horrible decision to have to institute.

"That's for really sick people. And people who can't do things for themselves," Ceci answered. I know she was crying inside. I just know it.

"Yes, Ceci. We know." I was crying on the outside.

We took with Ceci all the comforts we thought she might need at the Hospice home. My sister and I sewed sixty-three "C. O'Brien" tags in each of her personal articles the night before. This could not be happening. My sister would never need to live somewhere that you have to have name tags in all your clothes.

"Don't bring anything worth more than twenty or thirty dollars," the charge nurse said. What a kick. That really hit home. This was a facility we are taking my sister to. Ceci was going to a death institution. That was exactly what she feared back in August. She wondered then if she would have to go to a death institution. And here it was really happening to her. Oh, Gawd.

"We have night crawlers…roamers, we call them. They might take her things," the nurse continued on.

So we took her birthstone "Three Sisters" ring from her finger, her license—last piece of community living identification—her cash, and put it all in a safe place for her. And we left her with the allowable $13 in change. We put her things in a safe place but had grave doubts that we were putting her in a safe place. You couldn't just take all of someone's money when they have been independent a few days before. It was so harsh. It was their last touch with running-their-own-life days, with living their own lives. That is close to saying, "You can't take it with you." Oh. My. God.

Eighteen days after waking up a bit confused, we did put Ceci in another green-furnitured place. Ceci has always been a strong woman. "Going to outlive any grandchildren," people said. She exercised more than many of her friends, jogging miles a day.

*Entry*                                    *December 10*

*(Twenty-Two Days Before Diagnosis) – Ceci was still "with it"*

*Church group visited Bethesda Nursing Home today. Played Bingo with nine residents. Took them oatmeal cookies I baked last night. Cool morning. Made plans for boating this weekend with Barry and girls. Sun came out in the afternoon. Called Melanie. They are coming out this weekend to go to lunch at Kings Saturday. Called Carol and Doug to join us. Adam and I went to Belleview tonight for dinner. Ran two miles today and could have kept going. May sleet through the night. We go to the Nursing Home again next week—need to take four dozen cupcakes.*

# Where'd She Go?

"DON'T YOU AGREE, CECI?" the social worker said in Ceci's direction.

No response. My god. This was real. The social worker was talking to my sister and she was not responding. Where did she go? Reality was setting in for me. Slowly, sedated Ceci looked toward Deana, the social worker's end of the conference table and slowly focused her eyes somewhat below Deanna's face.

"Well, I know that's right," I responded for her. This was another step in realization. I was now doing her communication for her. To the final stages of her here-with-us-life, I spent much of my time with Ceci and others, responding as I knew my sister would or should. "Thank you for visiting us," I would say when the visitor did not know me.

# Lord, Lord Listen

DECEMBER 30 AND AGAIN on January 1 post-surgery, Ceci started a new journal. This one—not like the other annual journals she had kept—this one contained only entries of medically related issues.

*JANUARY 1, One Year Previous*     *JOURNAL ENTRY*

*Went to church service early this morning. I was awake till 9:30 last night. Didn't make it up to see the clock turn on the New Year. Didn't sleep much. Clarey and Barry took me to Aunt Melanie's for New Year's dinner. Amazing, a New Year turns over and the skies are like last year, calm. Hope it is a precursor of the new year. No resolutions needed—life is good!*

*JANUARY 1, One Year Later*

*Took headache tablet at 6:00. Took all 6:00 a.m. Noon I took a swelling go down at 12 noon. Antibiotic pill at noon. Nerve pill due*

*3:15 p.m. can be today. Nerve pill taken at
3:00 p.m.*

She even tried to keep track of some personal financial
bookwork these days, pay our insurance premium and figure her checkbook. Her writing was surprisingly very well
done. She was doing well at that point, one day post-op,
but after that the entries were in my sister's or her caretaker's handwriting.

*JOURNAL ENTRY*

*January 10*

*Ceci did not sleep well, only 2 1/2 hours
through the night. Meds given to her at
5:15 a.m. at her demand. Restless. Pacing
the floor. Ate a small amount of Cream of
Wheat for breakfast. Had to stop her from
taking the milk carton outside—insisted.
Wants to call the doctor and talk.*

# Did I Mention Anxiety?

IMAGINE THE BUSIEST DAY of your life. Now imagine a time when you have experienced extreme nervousness over an event or action—the kind where you feel your heart move up against your rib cage, close to your throat enough to make a little vomit begin to form, where your breathing is something so loud your blood-filled ears become conscious of it. Your ears have a certain hot sensation deep inside as if they are overheated and dangling from the sides of your head, held only by a tightening band. Cheekbones burn deep on the inside back near your constricting throat, and the room you are in is not there, but there is a pale aqua grey fog surrounding you. It's as if you can feel your thyroid working. That was me. Now add knowing there is terminal cancer in your body. Tie all this together and call it knowing-that-death-is-near anxiety. This, along with the inability to control any of these because of the post-brain-operation effects and disease related symptoms. And synthetic drugs and steroids are marching like soldiers through the cells that control things; these things caused tremendous bursting anxiety to deal with. Ceci began putting on twenty miles of fast-paced walking a day in the Hospice home, running laps along the halls of each corridor. She walked so much that her weakened little legs cramped terribly when she tried to rest. She eventually got strong enough to go out the door of the Hospice home and run away. She went to a nearby grocery store and a shopping plaza a quarter mile from the Hospice home. She walked there twice a day, unapproved and mostly unnoticed by staff.

My phone never stopped ringing—at home and at work.

"I saw your sister today," the caller would say.

Silence. Mine.

"Oh, were you at the Hospice home?" I would finally ask. Ha. I knew they weren't.

The doctor was not seeing to Ceci's needs. Hospice did not see to her needs. My sister and I saw to some of her basic requests—bring in her grade cards and card table, get an extra chair for her room.

The Hospice home staff did not see to her needs beyond, "Here's a pill (two hours late)," or "I'm here to scrub your floor, and you have too much junk in your room." God knows, Ceci could not see to her own needs. She was institutionalized in a nursing home for Hospice, having been found unable to function outside of a supervised facility and close to dying.

From the Dying Person's Bill of Rights: "I have the right to be treated as a living human being until I die."

I spent every spare minute beside Ceci, seeing to her needs as best anyone could another's needs. I ran myself ragged and worn. We spent money on every service, every phone call for help, on groceries, and prepared food to supplement her Hospice nursing home rations. I tried to see to her needs. I pleaded with her doctors and her nurses to discontinue a med, give her a med, and give her an antidote for the side effect of the last med, give her the extra food brought in for her, give her the extra food you said to request.

The desire to "do something" is common among everyone who has a family member or friend who has cancer or is dying.

There is nothing you can do to change the course, so you do everything you can for the person but, you can rarely see to their real need. We gave her all we could: understanding, hope, respect, things, and love but never touched her real need. The real need—the only need—was to escape the cancer. We couldn't see to that need.

From the Dying Person's Bill of Rights: "I have the right to be cared for by caring, sensitive, knowledgeable people who will attempt to understand my needs and will be able to gain some satisfaction in helping me face my death."

One of the worse parts of knowing you are dying soon has got to be (this has never happened to me, so I speak not from experience) the anxiety and depression. Let me repeat this for impact. Two of the worst aspects of nearing death are dealing with knowing you are dying and the torn emotions that lead to the most extreme anxietal behavior. The serotonin and other chemicals up there must be going through hell too.

In the Hospice care facility, Ceci went through a depression of the realization of leaving this world. She tried to starve herself to death by not eating. She weakened greatly over a week's time. She had actually come close to imagining a way to do herself in while in a nursing home! You don't hear of that much. But if you could canvas the unresponsive cadavers-in-waiting, betcha most want suicide.

Our Uncle Larry had been trying to convince Ceci to eat and that she could eat anything she wanted now. Not saying, "You are going to die anyway," but trying to surpass those words in the convincement. She was getting skinnier and skinnier post-op. She was not only trying to starve herself, but she was actually losing weight from all the bodily trauma, post-op loss of appetite, depression, a dislike of nursing home food and the lack of sense of taste and smell because of the tumors. Who would want to eat!

"Cec, we will bring you any food you want. Do you want chips? Aunt Meg's oatmeal cookies? Some of the Key Lime pie you love? And on and on, he went with food. "Why don't you eat the pudding they brought to you?"

"I don't want it," she replied.

"But you have always liked this before."

"I don't like to eat it."

"What don't you like about it?" Larry probed.

"It has cholesterol."

"Ceci, I have to tell you that this shouldn't matter to you anymore. Cholesterol can't hurt you anymore at this point in your illness. It won't hurt you."

"But I don't want cholesterol."

"Well, Ceci, you are going to die and eating cholesterol can't do you any further harm. You love butterscotch pudding. Eating the pudding would be good for you. We would bring you any food you like the taste of—just name it. You need to eat to get some strength from food."

"Well, I'm not going to eat cholesterol."

"Okay," Larry started. "We won't bring food with cholesterol. But whatever you eat cannot hurt you. You can eat anything you want. What would you like? You can have things with eggs in them. You can now have all the carbs you want. You can have some of the foods you haven't eaten in years because you were eating only healthy foods."

"I'm not going to eat it because I hate the taste of cholesterol."

"Ceci, that's okay. Think of some foods you would like to eat because we will make or bake and bring you anything. It doesn't matter if it is fattening. You are skinny. It doesn't matter if it has cholesterol. Why won't you eat these things?"

"I hate the taste of cholesterol. It tastes like sardines."

"Oh, I can't argue with that logic," Larry finally uttered, defeated.

She really wanted to die quickly. Several doctors and nurses explained to her about the sickening symptoms of dying in this manner, and eventually, another uncle, an internist in a geriatric facility, got the understanding through to Ceci about the grace of dying. She would be giving up the grace in dying. She started to eat to gain strength to fight—to fight us, rather than to fight the disease. Whatever it took. Good. You go, Ceci. Eat.

Anxiety took over whenever depression was not symptomatic. Even under strong medicinal control, these symptoms shone through like a burgeoning zit. She wanted her scrapbooking supplies and her grade recording book brought to her.

From the Dying Person's Rights: "I have a right to attempt to 'put my house in order' by myself."

Well, we got everything moved to the care facility and set up for her. We turned the lamp shade upside down at her request so that the light was more direct on her grade book. Everyone entering her room beyond that point thought she was crazy just seeing that upside down lampshade. We brought her all the things and she proceeded to "make noise" (her mental thesaurus word for keeping busy these days).

Bless her heart.

"Bless her heart." You've heard that joke…southern women can say anything about anyone as long as they follow it with, "Bless her heart." Look at the poor giant wart on her face, bless her heart. Her husband can't stand the way she nags and spends his money, bless her heart. It is no longer a nice phrase in my vocabulary.

Then they took my sister's scissors.

"She spoke of suicide by not eating, so we have to deal with each threat as sincere. We handle our patients with appropriate precautionary measures," said the evening supervisor on duty to me. "So we took her scissors as a safety measure."

So Ceci ran away again from the Hospice Home.

She ran to a local store a quarter mile away and bought herself, with another of the $13 ration of allowance, some scissors and a huge bottle of aspirin—five hundred pills. She wanted scissors to scrapbook with and the aspirin to be "something I could take to make this go away."

# Five Birthday Cards

As POWER OF ATTORNEY over Ceci's finances, I continued to give her an allowance. One week, she spent her $13 allowable about three times lying flat in her nursing home bed. "Night roamers" took it, more likely.

"Ceci, the money is yours to spend, but I just wondered what you bought today from your bed?" I was worried that maybe someone was pilfering as we had been warned by nursing staff.

"Well, I sent Tim $5 for his birthday," she told me.

Yes, she was sending cards and letters out. She was writing to everyone. She was writing last letters to her school students, aunts, uncles, and was sending out early Valentines to our little cousins. I bought her a fancy box of valentines to send, but she wanted to make some. God bless her soul and her endurance. And her fortitude. She took her strength and will to communicate to her pencil. The notes were strong in meaning to each, but most unintelligible, repetitious, and slanted in script. Father Tim did get a birthday card with $5 in it from Ceci. And another. And another. Day after day.

# Let Me Pray

THERE WERE NO MASSES held at nursing/Hospice home. A rosary service was held once each Friday when Sister Claris could make it. Father O'Malley was not on assignment to make visits to the Hospice home. Huh! Ceci had prayed every morning, night and day of her before-cancer life. Now, she was stricken not only with cancer but denial of the right to worship.

She walked in to the Hospice home chapel during a congregational service.

"You can't come in here, Ceci," the lay minister told her.

A Hospice home aid helped her to turn around and headed her back out the chapel door.

"I just wanted to pray with you," Ceci softly told the minister as she was being spun around.

"But this is a congregational service and you are Catholic, ma'am," the aide told her. Ma'am? Ma'am? Ceci did look old. Part of her hair was shaved, part cut by her; unkempt and drawn was her style now and she looked aged. No twinkle in her eye, trouble with each step, and that look—that look of standing three fields away from anywhere with no facial affect.

She just wanted to pray.

From the Dying Person's Bill of Rights: "I have the right to discuss and enlarge my religious and/or spiritual experiences whatever these may mean to others."

# Bless Your Heart

AUNT TOOTSY, BLESS HER heart.

Did you know also you could so be absolved from saying anything bad about anyone if you said, "Bless their heart" after it? (Not true.)

People brought Ceci yarn art kits like she was six. People tried to get her to try chemotherapy. "Is anyone seeing to your need for chemotherapy?" they would ask. Goddammit. No, hell, no. No, we are not doing anything to try to make Ceci better. What do you think! We just want her to lie in this bed and do yarn art, *bless your heart.*

I told Barry, "Bless her heart, Aunt Tootsy thinks Cec can do yarn art."

He repeated, "Yes, Bless her heart." We smiled together at our shared joke. And then he held me a long time.

Let me reiterate: truth is, Dr. Eastern had immediately said her quality would remain better if we did not add chemo treatments to this grade of tumor or to the extensive post-op healing. Again ethics taught the doctor to never say, "There is nothing to be done." He offered, however, "If someone feels that there is a hope of more time, please proceed with a referral. I would give all notes and reports and offer consult. Time is all you will buy, perhaps not a more comfortable time," he added. Ouch.

Aunt Tootsy, *bless her heart*, told Ceci, "But there is always hope of cure."

"I know a case where…" Uncle Bernie shared with Cec, *bless his heart*.

Ceci would mumble, "Did they have brain cancer?" Dead silence. Let me repeat. Dead silence. But bless their hearts for trying.

The do-gooders in life know not what they do. Ceci heard more stories about death, dying, and cancer. Already in a breeding ground of germs and bacteria, add negative energy? *Why on earth* would someone dying want to hear of those morbid things! Gees, people, get a clue.

One night, taking off on these feelings inside, I was thinking of putting a sampler over Cec's bed that said. "If you want to talk about already dead people, my hearing went first." Barry and I took off on this with more, "My coffin is in the shop. Let's still talk about life." Or "I'm dying in mine. Tell me about your life." Or "If you tell me one more gallstone story, I'm outta here," or "Dead end."

I know we are sick to think like this. But put yourself in the room with someone dying for months—your sense of humor becomes distorted and your emotions want to break loose amok.

"Notice I am horizontal. Please speak in a low voice." Barry liked doing this too. We had morbid laughter. We were out of our own minds with worry. We were just plain out of our minds.

Sorry, but I was trying to think of how Ceci might want to die… Laughing on the way out or watching everyone with long faces regale sobbing stories of misery? I want her to remember our love, not our sadness. Come on, Ppeople.

We filled her ceiling with pictures of living—pictures of all of us in costumes, wearing a smiling face mask, pictures of her with Barry and other friends, all over the world together, her students. Enjoy these, sister. Forget about the people that want to talk about their illnesses and losses.

# I'm Going Home

REMARKABLY, THERE WERE STRONGER days mid-March, and we did get Ceci to Sunday mass each week. As we drove up to the Hospice home one Sunday morning, Ceci came out fully dressed in her winter coat and scarf, walking on her own, no aide. As she climbed agilely into my van, she announced, "Guess what, girls. I'm moving home tomorrow" with fake sincerity to the smile on her face. She emoted. We were aghast. Yeah, improvement. The trip to church that day, however, was sacrilegious. We were all upset with God and each other, and worrying about many things, not devout worship.

"Let's go have coffee and a giant cinnamon roll at Barry's," Clarey said after church.

Ceci refused, as she knew we would try to change her mind about moving home, but we drove her to Barry's anyway. Gol', it is so hard to be defiant to someone who is ill. It was of mutual consent but felt like an unconscious conspiracy against Ceci. Who did I think I was?

"Let's just go and talk," we said to Ceci as we pulled in Barry's driveway.

That was the day we told Ceci that she was crazy. It was the only way that it would concretely set in. She was afraid of being institutionalized and yet, here she already was. It was the only way she comprehended her circumstances—at least for that moment. Barry actually had the nerve more than us sisters to say to Ceci that she was doing things that were a danger to her and she needed to be watched constantly and closely medicated to stay alive.

Ceci asked him, "Do you mean I'm crazy?" And he had to answer that she was doing crazy things. That was a whole hell week in one day!

# 271 Cards

"I GOT 213 CARDS," Ceci announced as I arrived at the Hospice home.

And the sequential week—"I got 271 cards. I have lots of friends who can get me out of here," she offered as proof that she would find a way home.

Through all the insanities we thought we saw, Ceci was making the best sense that you possibly could, drawing from every fiber of her intelligence, through a brain that was demolished and deficit. She was rationalizing that if she had that many friends, surely one could help her escape from this, from this cancer. From this Hospice home. From this hell.

I, of course, through guilt, talked with her doctor about any therapy at this point. No. No. No. She would only die sooner should we put her through the trips, yet alone the radiation's biting decomposition of cells her body would never replace.

Oh.

# Family Meetings

THE FAMILY BEGAN TO have conference calls of all the Michigan siblings and outreach calls to the other family members, our grandmother, aunts and uncles involved, etc. We would meet as we could among two or three of us to make decisions about Ceci. Dr. Horrible (his name was really Houbill) finally said that Ceci could go home, and of course, Ceci wanted to go there more than anything.

But we felt we couldn't let that happen. It was too dangerous again. She was too wobbly, too confused, and very highly medicated, which we doubted we could manage. Eventually the family meetings were being held every four or five days. We discussed that Ceci did have the right to go home now if at all possible. Dr. Horrible ordered that we take her home when we could arrange to do so. I fought it. I couldn't stand the idea that we would take her home and then be responsible for a decision that would kill or harm her because she could either break a hip and be hospitalized again, or fall down the steps and kill herself, or perhaps run away and drown in the river, not that far from our home, or she may show up on some doorstep or God forbid—try to take her own life. All which would possibly end in death. Oh, my. Ceci might die by accident or on purpose instead of her illness. Hmmm. Oh my.

The best decision was for her to go back to a familiar environment and have as peaceful surroundings as could be provided for as long as could be provided, Dr. Horrible told us. That statement meant the beginning of the end—again. I knew it was the right thing to do, but I did not want it so. I did not want her at risk to herself. All I wanted was to stop this death. Taking her home was another step toward her demise. Again, helpless, I couldn't stop this. She was safer at home than in the Hospice home, maybe. Nursing staff hired at home could help regulate and supply her medication and assess her medication needs. They could feed her when it was meal time—on time— with hot food (not cooled institutional tray food) and they could monitor her so that she didn't have a seizure without being seen and they would know how to handle a seizing person and could account for her bruises and cuts from her falls and they could stop her from going the wrong way or running away, or running with scissors, or dying alone.

Gees. Where does my mind go when I worry? It was my own responsibility issues that wanted Ceci to stay in the Hospice home till death. In fact, when we did take her home, at my insistence, we paid (donated) for her Hospice bed to be held for three more weeks; I was so certain we could not manage her at her home.

We hired round-the-clock geriatric aides, the only type available for Ceci's list of needs. They were well qualified; after all, they had stayed with Mrs. Hrsuka's husband, Father Jamas, and Marie Collins when they each were dying. Oh. My. God. They came well qualified due to that? Helping someone to die?

Family took turns staying home with Ceci for three to five days a week. I took my turn. Sure, it may have helped her to have a comfier day in her home, but she couldn't be comfy anywhere. She had cancer.

JOURNAL NOTE     MARCH—the year of her death

*Doctor, what shall I do to help myself? Isn't there help to make me move or help move around move should I go out to do things. I was told I could be moving around, around what is it inside?*

*Jesus, what's going on again. I'm not good for anything. Ardene brought such a nice card and beautiful flitters which really taste good. I've never learned to make them. I hope I can. Save some of Doug and Carol to taste. Jesus, please make me mortal and wise to explain how nice they are*

Please, someone, help me and my sister.
Okay home again, home again.
Those first days at home, as lousy as they were, were more peaceful for Ceci. She went for walks outside, even twice one day, during her first few days at home. She started her day by attending mass a couple of days that first week at home. She had to have assistance to do each, but she was doing some things that were her normal. And she actually slept. She slept long hours. (Compared to the last few

weeks, a four-hour sleep was a long stint!) The meds were once again a challenge to learn. The doctor had cut her tranquilizer in hopes that once home, she would relax a bit and not need as much medicine to induce control over her anxiety. What a fool. Her anxiety rose in the first hour. She was wild upon arriving home. She raced wobbling from wall to wall, door to door, and out the front door. Clarey went running out the door after Cec.

Ceci fired her caretakers at least twice a week. They were really the sweetest, caring ladies helping her. In between firing them, Ceci begged us to make them go. She wanted to be left home alone to just die. I know she thought that if everyone left her alone, she might accomplish that on her own. You were probably right, Ceci, but that would have been neglectful and abusive. We couldn't do that. We couldn't do that in our hearts. We needed to stay with you. We needed to stay with you and help you eat. We had to see that you were bathed. We had to give you meds. We had to watch you so that you didn't get confused and burn the house down. We had to watch so that you didn't hurt yourself. We had to...but Ceci didn't want any of it.

As we were hiring the caretakers, Clarey made the statement in front of Ceci that Ceci was not able to do everything and needed help.

Ceci turned to Clarey and slapped her, saying, "Well, I never." It hurt Clarey. Oh, not in the physical sense, but it hurt Clarey. Ceci had not slapped Clarey since they were both small children and not heeding some warning to "not touch my stuff." The caretakers caught on that very moment as to what Ceci's illness was going to be like for them to manage. There was only a couple of other lashing-out instances, one of which was my fault, so one of the ladies was the recipient of another physical slap instead of me.

It was the second week at home. The first week, I got meds early in the week so the med pack was situated: SMTWTFS. I thought the med pack ran from Monday through Sunday. I was wrong. That Sunday morning before 6:00 a.m., the night caretaker tapped on my door. "We're out of the anxiety med," the caretaker said behind the door to not upset Ceci further.

I dashed to the Hospice home donning my jeans over my pj's and not even combing my hair. Luckily, they had not returned Cec's meds to the pharmacy, and the night nurse illegally handed me her Hospice home meds. I arrived within twenty minutes back at the house since the sudden wake up call. Ceci had gotten up, however, at 5:00 a.m. and needed her morning antianxiety med desperately. She had already pulled Donna's hair and stomped on Donna's foot. Donna had called the other caretaker too. The ladies had shown Ceci the empty container and told her I was on the way home, but nothing could restrain the anxiety Cec was having—nothing. I felt worse about the fact that Ceci had to experience this, even though I felt awful for not realizing how the med week ran and for Donna's foot and hair but worst that Ceci was going through a higher level of hell than she would have had to with the med. Donna was very forgiving. Ceci had never ever done anything in her life anywhere near saying something negative behind someone's back, yet alone assault a human! She didn't even kill mice; she set them free.

And Ceci somehow recognized I had a part in the reason for the altercation. I am not sure she understood what had taken place, that she was anxious or that she had hurt Donna, but she did know that she was mad at me. And that lasted three days. When I saw her again later the same day of the incident, she was still upset with me and it took her that long to forget. I guess I was lucky that she was forgetting some things these days.

# When the Shaking Started

SOMETHING IN ALL OF this brain tumor madness started Ceci shaking. In her years before near-death, she had never been shaky. She had been able to do any fine motor skill, distribute communion, teach, bake, pick up tiny beads in art projects, garden, hold on to rappelling ropes, etc. before now. Before March-near-death days. A more scientific observation would be that the tumor was leaking into other lobes, which disciplined actions, sense, and thoughts.

She got shakier and shakier. Her legs were wobbling carrying her swollen, heavier but frail body. Something was working on her nervous system.

There were other signs. As we looked back at the story of the progression of the cancer, we could see significant changes that led us to believe the cancer was back and actively growing. We always wanted to believe that it was some other thing, not driven by her brain cancer—a side effect maybe, maybe it would go away. But very little was going away these days. More just kept coming and coming. And Ceci knew it too. She said she was shakier. Some days would be slightly better, but then the next would be double movement of two days ago. It was strange how this acted. What isn't strange about cancer?

Ceci cognitively asked, "When is my funeral anyway?" just after Sunday mass.

Barry had carried Ceci up the St. Patrick's steps so that she could attend. Ceci gleaned over the words in the church bulletin as if studying them. I wondered if she was actually reading at the kitchen table with the church bulletin in front of her face.

"Where is…" she said. "Where is my funeral date in here?" she asked looking at Clarey.

We all knew we were getting closer to that. Her last two rides would be by ambulance and a hearse.

Good Friday arrived.

I think Ceci actually believed that she was going to die on Good Friday. She slept off and on that day, as naps were more frequent again for her, and she lost track of the time of day or night upon awakening. Somehow, I believe she had her "dying" so associated with the fact that Good Friday was a day of death, hers if she could arrange it. That, and the fact that the doctor had told her she had three to four months to live back in December. That made Good Friday or April 17 the fourth month. She woke up after midnight actually on that Saturday morning after Good Friday and said very enthusiastically, "Happy Easter!" to Clarey as Clarey struggled to open her eyes with the bright light behind Ceci coming in through the blinds.

"Happy Easter," Ceci said again. She was more delighted with the fact that she arose than the fact that it was actually Easter Saturday. We were delighted too, Ceci. More than you know. We were delighted with the risen Ceci on Saturday and the risen Christ on Sunday!

The edema in her face was really noticeable these days. She had very swollen cheeks and her eye focus seemed worsening every three or four days. She sat half an hour in a chrome kitchen type chair, and we noticed that her legs and feet turned very purple from the circulation happening or not happening in that short time. She had to be pushed to bathe several times when she was up during the day. Sometimes she was able to bathe herself and groom herself along (although we know she put hairspray under her arms instead of deodorant). The meds were making her eat voraciously and her stomach was rapidly engorging.

# I'm Never Again Telling You a Thing!

BLISTERS ON HER TONGUE meant one thing. White pimples on her tongue meant another. Bleeding sores, a third change. Just when we thought we knew how to respond to the symptoms, new side effects and symptoms would occur or meds would be changed. Dr. Horrible adjusted her Cortisone to lessen the edema build up in her cheeks and apparently rid her of the most recent white pimples with bleeding. Gees.

Cortisone, while holding back the swelling which effected tumor growth and ultimately her behavior, abilities, and mental capacity, also changed other bodily functions and prevalent occurrences. New infections occurred. Resistance to dosages occurred. We were told a med could prolong a coma and cause gastrointestinal bleeding or pneumonia. Prolonged use could cause damage to the optic nerve and vision. Gees, God?

We had noticed the first sores and talked to Ceci about getting some new med for them. So Ceci realized we were watching her symptoms as we made her rinse her mouth or that we called the doctor or changed her routine of medicines for the day in some way. So Ceci responded with, "I'm never telling you a thing." So the symptoms and signs of pains and aches and bleeding that were not visible became her secret. She didn't want us tending to her or changing meds or messing with her. If she had sores on her tongue again, she never told us.

Trying to do a little at home mental assessment with a nurse and social worker, a blood pressure check and some other physical tests were administered to Ceci. While Clarey held three fingers straight out in different directions—up, down, and side to side—from a distance, I held a card over one of Ceci's eyes.

"Which way do my fingers go?" Clarey asked.

"Three going south," Ceci replied at seeing Clarey's down-pointed fingers. Ceci's eyesight that day was doing pretty well. She did scrawl her name on a couple of greeting cards to send out to relatives, a card of thanks and a baby congratulations card for the newest namesake infant cousins, to one of the five of her girlfriends who were expecting children that year.

She even read a brief printed prayer and perused her mail this week. The ability came and went for Ceci more and more often, as did the ability to focus attention on the written passage. Panic anxiety even interfered with her ability to interpret cognizably what she read or concentrate on the words long enough to understand them or hold a page or a book in front of her eyes. Anxiety is weird stuff, whether it is you feeling it or watching someone else go through it.

Dr. Hagar the Horrible did all the wrong things for all the wrong reasons. Or so we thought. He overmedicated Ceci. He undertreated. He didn't listen to us. He undermedicated. He believed what Ceci told him in her confused state! He said the family was uncaring. He wouldn't work with the Hospice people whose only job was to make Ceci comfortable. He wouldn't work with the oncologist. He told my sister to her face that she either had seven minutes or seven weeks to live. (Great, Doc. Now you go home and sleep tonight. We will all stay up and deal with Ceci's anxiety over *that* news while she runs up and down the stairs, out of the Hospice home door, and we will deal with her flailing and her new rash and her added pain.)

"God, if you are real and out there, please help us," Clarey and I cried together.

She had more and more severe seizures that night.

# I Need My Pills Now

Looking back and ahead:

Don't change the pain med.
Switch antibiotic drug.
Stop Polymox.
Start Ceclor.
Start antidepressant and Amitriptyline.
Alter anxiety med.
Remain on blood pressure med.
Switch doctors.
Stop the Dexamethason because of complications.
Decadron caused hallucinations.
Hospice involvement allows unlimited meds.
Doctor disagrees.
Doctors disagree.
Meds disagree with patient.
Sores on tongue as reaction to medication.
Allergic to Tetracycline.
Add Aspirin.
No Aspirin.
Trial of Lorazapam.
One doctor prefers Salsalate.
Colace three times a day.

Dulcolax now needed for constipation.
Roxicet for pain every 6 hours.
Increase Lorazapam.
Decrease Lorazapam.
Color code the med packs.
Up her antidepressant.
More depression.
Anxiety.
Seizures.
Morphine every two hours.

WHATEVER THE MED, IT was synthetic. Man made. Man-made chemicals to try to make my sister's body naturally live while she was dying. What irony.

Hospitalization happened again. More IVs.

Ceci pulled out her oxygen tubes repeatedly on that Thursday. She pulled at her IVs trying to pull the needles out of her arms. We had been gone from the room only seconds. The next day, she pulled her catheter out as well. Did she know what she was doing subconsciously? Did she know that taking these out would cause her sooner death?

Dr. Horrible told us that day, "We will not reinsert the IV. Of course, this must be a unified family decision, but my decision is to not put her on IV drugs or solutions again. Contact all family members and let me know." That was all he had to say. The formality of it. Jesus.

The hardest decision making I have ever been in on. That is just how the cold real world operates; it is a business when death starts.

# You Have Four Cavities

THE WEEKEND ON-CALL PHYSICIAN and I worked five minutes to get Ceci to open her mouth. She had not even had ice chips all Saturday. For the first time since her post-op days, she was not able to awaken enough to swallow for us. The ice chips melted on her closed lips and began to dribble down her cheeks and in her chin crevice.

"Wake up, Ceci. The doctor needs to see your tongue," I said coaxing, at my dying sister's ear.

She had once again developed huge festering blisters as a reaction to one of the drugs she had been ingesting. After five minutes of prodding and begging, Ceci finally opened her mouth enough for the doctor to see the tip of her tongue and examine the blisters to prescribe yet another medicine to counter this new hell going on inside her body.

Later that day, she actually rallied a bit from the coma-like status. Unfortunately or not, dietary had not caught up with nurses' directives and brought a tray. Ceci was not eating, but actually that morning "came to" and maybe had ten bites of lunch and drank a little cream soup from the wronged tray, and then she did respond to the afternoon nurse on her request to again see Cec's tongue.

"Open your mouth, Ceci. We need to see your tongue," the nurse asked upon doctor's order.

"Can you stick out your tongue Ceci, for me?" Clarey pleaded.

"Can you open wide like this?" the nurse demonstrated directly over Ceci's now-open eyes.

Barely opening her mouth, not wide enough for the sought exam, Ceci said, "You have four cavities," to the nurse. The family and the nurse were nearly rolling on the floor for the next five minutes. Stress relief. Thanks, Ceci.

# Receiving God

SOMETHING MIRACULOUS HAPPENED. NOT once, but twice.

Ceci gave herself up to God. He, by evidence I'd say, invited her in, and we were fortunate to observe the sacrament. It happened a day before Ceci died. Ceci had been quite sedated and unresponsive, but as if strength came from her soul during her comatose status, eyes closed, she slowly lifted first one arm and then the other, straight up toward the ceiling, in a worshipping pose with palms formed like Mary's in giving, from her prone position on the whiteness of the hospital bed. She paused, her arms held there moments before putting both arms down simultaneously, slowly in a gentle, muscle-less fall, to her sides. Without a word. It was awesome. Everyone knew what we had seen in their very core.

She did it one more time before she died—from a coma state again.

The day that my sister Ceci did this, the newspapers ran a story of people reporting the vision of a miracle in our state's capitol, not far from the hospital. They saw a colorful display in the sun believed to have been a sign from the Virgin Mary. It has been seen periodically since 1917, like a host, a communion wafer spinning with vibrant colors shooting out of it. Witnesses reported feeling glorious.

Ceci had asked us to go home all the time. She was plugged into all sorts of hospital contraptions from every orifice and some holes surgically made. She had asked everyone to take her home, to cut it out of her, and then to take her on home. "Can you help me to get it out?" she would ask. And then "I am trying to get there," she would say. "Do you have a bus?" she pulled at us. Then she went comatose. I had a flinch of a thought that she was trying to go home to Heaven.

Her blood pressure was quite high. Weirdly high. By the time the nurses got an oxygen level and meds in her blood stream, she was showing pneumonia-like symptoms—in minutes, I swear. There were tremors, clamminess, extreme chest rasping, and congestion, coughing, stomach bloating. That is so traumatic for a body to go through.

And all I could do was stand here. Dammit. Just let her have peace. I held her hand.

There I said it. The peace of dying. Dying. Does dying have to be so hard on her?

The ICU nurse says to Clarey, "I understand she has an Advance Directive." Very first words out of her mouth, I swear. Was this really most important to you? Better go take Dr. Eastern's Ethic's Class 101. Advance Directive as your first question about my loved one? I mean, really.

Oh God. Ceci's left hand went up. Straight up in the air from her prone position on the bed. Then her right hand and arm followed. She held them there for many minutes. We knew she was physically not able to do that. She was too weak. That, and she was still comatose.

In that moment, Ceci gave herself up to God. He invited her in, and we observed this sacrament. It happened a minute before she died. It was as if strength came from her soul to hold her arms up. Without a whimper or a word, her arms came down simultaneously at her sides. It was awesome, her passing. We knew. We just knew.

I am still her sister. I will always be that. But now one of us is physically no more. I have her only in memory. She is gone from this planet.

# Post-Death

WHAT A HORRIBLE TITLE to a book section.

Ceci had said she wanted to go home. That was the last bit of her oration we will ever hear. She said it plainly but not opening her eyes. All the while we thought she meant our house. She wanted a bus, a horse—anything to take her to death.

I think that we did *everything* we knew to do for my sister, as did her doctors. There is always that nagging thought of "if only," however.

The only "if only" I know of is this: "If only she could have lived forever for me."

Catch yourself. Do you believe that tomorrow stretches forever?

In reflection after her death, I suppose God did know and he did give us a warning of what was to come. He gave us some time to say goodbye before death took her away from this physical life. I certainly attrited a long way from my pre-novice application days to a doubting Christian during Ceci's slow death. I found I was preparing for the outcome of Ceci's illness but not for my life post-Cec.

I hope that I offered you the vision to see each day as precious, each sunset as an event, each 24 hours as a gift to be used completely for important stuff, not the urgent stuff.

*I am standing upon the seashore.*
*A ship at my side spreads her white*
*sails to the morning breeze*
*And starts for the blue ocean.*
*She is an object of beauty and strength.*
*I stand and watch her until at length she hangs*
*Like a speck of white cloud*
*Just where the sea and the sky come to mingle with each other*
*Then someone at my side says: "There, she is gone."*
*"Gone where?"*
*"Gone from my sight.*
*That is all."*
*She is just as large in mast and hull and spar as she was*
*When she left my side*
*And she is able to bear her load of living*
*freight to her destined port.*
*Her diminished size is in me, not in her.*
*And just at the moment when someone at my side says,*
*"There, she is gone!"*
*There are other eyes watching her coming,*
*And other voices ready to take up the glad shout:*
*"Here she comes!"*

—Henry Van Dyke

# Hospice, Inc.

## The Dying Person's Bill of Rights

I HAVE THE RIGHT to be treated as a living human being until I die.

I have the right to maintain a sense of hopefulness however changing its focus may be.

I have the right to be cared for by those who can maintain a sense of hopefulness, however changing this might be.

I have the right to express my feelings and emotions about my approaching death in my own way.

I have the right to participate in decisions concerning my care.

I have the right to expect continuing medical and nursing attention even though "cure" goals must be changed to "comfort" goals.

I have the right not to die alone.

I have the right to be free from pain.

I have the right to have my questions answered honestly.

I have the right not to be deceived.

I have the right to have help from and for my family in accepting my death.

I have the right to die in peace and dignity.

I have the right to retain my individuality and not be judged for my decisions which may be contrary to beliefs of others.

I have the right to discuss and enlarge my religious and/or spiritual experiences whatever these may mean to others.

I have the right to expect that the sanctity of the human body will be respected after death.

I have the right to be cared for by caring, sensitive, knowledgeable people who will attempt to understand my needs and will be able to gain some satisfaction in helping me face my death. Yuck

# *Yuck*

So WHEN WE DID our last tripod with one leg up in heaven with the casket, the picture of heaven I had was of northern lights. I hope Ceci was going directly from being held in our arms to the arms of Jesus, just like she described her vision of heaven that night watching northern lights. I would like to think that. I would like to think that she is infinitely happy in a bliss of northern light clouds and extremely comfortable. For comfort is the opposite of what she has had the last few months.

Today is the one-month anniversary of Ceci's passing. Today is hard. Each day, each task in the process of picking up the pieces of my life has been hard. With the unbelievable compassion of friends and undying love of relatives, I awaken to realize that Ceci was not the only person in my life. She was a huge part of my existence of my blood; she taught me much, she showed me the world, she saw to many of my needs. I had to come face to face with the fact of having that one person missing from my life *and* still having all the other persons who are dear to me around me. That reminds a person that you are among the living and can cope, and that you can have your life back after their death. Never the same though.

After her death, we read more diary entries.

Ceci's Diary Entry                December 6

*Almost sick. Went to school (She didn't.)*
*Packages are ready for Christmas but I*
*baked two dozen cookies to put in school*
*boxes. Tired.*

She had been sick for longer than we knew, she had known she was just not right and had probably thought about her fatality more than we did. She was probably prepared and ready to meet God. Boy, that adjustment takes a while for those left living.

I spent two months crying and five years in pain of her death. Reflections tell me we couldn't have done any more. Ceci had lived a good life, but I am ill… I am sick with heartache.

My only "if only" is this: "If only she could have lived forever."

My new sampler is: "Catch yourself. Do you believe that tomorrow stretches forever?"

I never thought I could live after Ceci died.

The Sunday after Easter, Father Tom (not the bartender) asked us why we try to hold onto the dead. It woke me from my Sunday morning church-in-rote stupor. He went on to list my reasons:

1. Our security
2. Our identification with them
3. The love they gave us
4. Respect for the person they were in our lives

"These—these are all our own wants," he went on. "We don't get to control or understand God's plan. Only He knows the past and the future truth and will lead us. Are you living in that truth or stuck on the failure to receive your *wants*?" Ouch.

I didn't want to take a breath or a step without Ceci in my world. My parents dying didn't affect me that hard, but I was so young when they passed. Ceci was everything to me, to us, to our apposed tripod. I had Ceci longer than I had my parents in my life.

# *Me*

THIS IS TO LET you know there is life after death. I was certain two months prior to Ceci's death, two weeks prior to her death, and two days prior to her death that once she passed away, I could not ever know "normal" again, that I would want to die too because to live without her is not for me. I believed that. I wondered how I would cope, if I could cope. I wondered what kind of basket case I would be. Really. I told Barry when he asked how I was that I would like someone to just find a wheelchair and push me around the rest of my life because my emotions were so fragile and my heart was breaking, there was no way I could ever again act or be a normal responsible person.

But...

I knew I could experience grief and not stay in despair.

It took a while... It had taken me five years to wake up. I moved through the motions of life in a state of cloudy-brained slumber of job, fun, family picnics, driving down the road, eating, sleeping, attending family graduations, weddings, a trip to Europe, WalMart shopping, snow-skiing with Barry and Ceci's gang, grandma's death, writing my thesis for my doctorate, snorkeling off Catalina, and cooking classes. I even had a boyfriend, Drake, for five months. I just moved through the motions, not awake. To lose someone like Ceci, it takes a while to come back to good health emotionally and psychologically. God was not even really present for me during those five years. Clarey dragged me to church a few times. I rotely repeated the mass responses and even sang strongly with the choir, but I wasn't present. It was all surreal. I was a floating Margo above the events, the calendar days passing by. Tours of Italy, Breckenridge, Los Angeles, were all just spots on the geography of earth. I was above the world, like on a non-magic carpet seeing life going by but not experiencing it. It was like reading a book about my life but not being in it. I floated above the flowers I sniffed with a thickness in my perceptions, above the computer when I worked, above the bed when I made love with Drake. I never enjoyed it. For five years. Imagine. I was experiencing it, but not absorbing the exuberance of life.

Then I woke up one morning having a coke at Ceci's favorite tenderloin place. Carrie, the waitress, put two cherries in my cherry coke and the flavor was never more distinct ever before in my life. I woke up. The fellow next to me was discussing the defamation of a church he had just read about in the newspaper while with his breakfast mate.

I thought, *How awful to deface a church*, and I was thinking of the bisque statue of Immaculate Mary with its glow of blue light that I had really seen for the first time at the novice orientation, sacred from storms and vandals. Deep in my mind, I said an unconscious involuntary prayer that St. Catherine's church was all right, and that it was not the church which was being discussed. All of a sudden, I realized the man with the newspaper was wearing the same cologne that my father wore. I think it was the first time in five years that I smelled anything. It was so acute. My "Amen," a memory of Dad's scent, and the cherry in the coke woke me up. Gees. I was amazed that I was involuntarily praying. I could smell and taste again. Where was I for five years?

Sick with grief.

A grief counselor had told me in a group that some of us stay in masochistic grief, attached to a relentless pursuit of the bad. Some of us have dawning recognition that we get to accept and move on. That is what is happening. The latter is what I experienced the day having a fountain coke.

# Really Grown Up/I Can Leave a Legacy Now

I MATURED SOME DURING my post-traumatic antiadrenaline stage of grief.

We had evolved. Clarey seemed to come out of her numbness more quickly than I, and she got involved with life again just months after Ceci passed. She often spoke of Ceci's life, our many stories together, and Ceci's quirks as if Ceci was still with us. She could talk about it like that. She could laugh and smile about the many good times we all had with Ceci. I hadn't been able to. I was just numb and sad for a long, long time. The mention of Ceci's name now always made my heart skip at least one beat, and I froze inside. "Ceci." The room spun, and I stood motionless. Her absence was stronger than any other feeling.

God's design—destiny, whatever you call it—was definitely set for Clarey and me. God saw to it that we had been there for Ceci when she was ill. We had no conflicting distractions pining for our care or affection, no children yet, or significant others. He waited to give us boyfriends and husbands until after Ceci was gone. I'm sure He was fair to us all in that. Since we didn't have parents, it was only right that Clarey and I had been there with all our love and support for Cec. It added, in retrospect, a fairness in life.

I comprehend the cosmic proportions of birth and death and Heaven's glory. But acceptance in my own heart and head were slow in coming. Fortunately, other family and friends had carried me along.

Barry and I continued to hang out after Ceci died, almost exclusive friends; we needed each other. Clarey started dating pretty consistently this Gary fellow. "Gary and Clarey." We teased them that they couldn't be a couple because their names sounded too silly. We all had a fine time together. I managed to not bring down all the gaiety. I could just go along with life, but mostly feeling like I wasn't participating. I would just smile and laugh as expected. But I just wasn't experiencing my old joy—for a long time.

Gary and Clarey, and Barry (tee hee) and I made some major memories regardless of my state of mind in those five years. We toured Northern Europe, went to a gay wedding in LA, helped with the hurricane clean up through Red Cross in New Orleans, and hiked Lake Michigan's many trails of water falls, and river rafted in Colorado. When I look back at all of the pictures, it is all surreal—I just couldn't live life back then. God must have needed me to mourn that long so that I would have a comparison for the later happiness he intended to give me for the rest of my days.

Anyway, I hoped so.

Funny that it took a cherry coke and Dad's cologne to get me back. And Barry and Clarey's undying love.

# Clarey Deserves It

IT WAS INTERESTING THAT, to the day of Ceci admitting she was confused which led to the discovery of her brain tumor, one year to the day—Gary entered our lives. He was in the same emergency room slot as Ceci had been. He had her brunette hair color and those intriguing sharp green eyes like Ceci. Clarey was Gary's nurse. The trauma unit was full, and she got called down to assist from the post-op unit she was working.

Immediately, they were friends. That moment. Clarey teased Gary that maybe his hernia was a third testicle manifesting itself. He tried to laugh and shrugged into pain. Well, she was looking at his underwear-less groin. She was the epitome of caring, empathetic, and sincere with her patients. And Gary responded. He asked for morphine, and she held his hand through the pain. He said, "I'll rip your hand off." He moaned.

"If you can grow a third testicle, maybe I can grow another hand," Clarey responded to him.

After morphine, Gary softly said, "I'll take your offer of your hand." She walked him up to surgery and was back in post-op when he came out, to hold his hand when he awoke as she promised.

He said, "You're still here."

She said, "I'm not going anywhere." And that was it. And six months later, he really asked for her hand—in marriage.

Clarey swears, it was love when first their green Irish eyes met.

Gary loved Clarey, there was no doubt. So that was it. She started wedding planning in just a few months. I say *she* because Gary felt it best to stay out of it, standing back and okaying everything and I mean everything, Clarey mentioned. It became a little hard for Clarey to do because he was such an "Okay" man instead of offering his opinion. I guess that sort of set the precursor for their marriage. She got to do more in life with Gary's advocate and support. He loved not just her but her everything—every whim, every dream, every idea. I didn't think anyone other than the three of us sisters could love like that, but I was very glad that my sister had found it. I could see that love between them. I could recognize it, but I couldn't love like that, after Ceci, the strongest of loves, got pulled from my life or so I thought.

God had ruined me for that or so I thought.

*Okay, there,* I said it out loud, or in my thoughts out loud anyway. I was blaming God. It was that moment that I realized I was blaming God for Ceci's death instead of loving him. Here Gary was loving Clarey like no one else unrelated I knew had ever loved another, more than my parents loved. I could recognize that, and I could compare it because of my almost-novice intelligence. I had moved from loving God to blaming him. It was a habit after five years. Woo, what a moment. You know those driving-down-the-road-alone moments when you *get* something, the lightning bolt strikes, that old adage shows its meaning, the green in the grass is brighter, when what your mom said sinks in, when the words of a song finally are heard—that kind of a moment. Like when the words of the song are, "Going to the Chapel and we're gonna…" instead of "Going to a jack-o-lantern… Gonna get maaarrried." Cherry coke was my turning point.

And they were married.

With Gary, Clarey's husband, love, honor, and obey were facts. In that promise, love is a given, we all know "obey" is now a joke our ancestors threw in the vows, and honor is a most weighted word between two people. Most of us are all basically too selfish to actually show honor—yes, even to a spouse! Gary, he honored Clarey. She came first. What she valued, he showed value to; what she cared for, he caressed and held precious; what she did, he watched and supported; you know—honor. I was beginning to understand how to love more, honor, and have God again warm up my every moment. Funny how God set me up. I had to know about death being the end of life. I had to learn about love between couples. I had to know sadness and understand that there was an opposite of sadness[*]. I had to know an empty life to cherish the full one only God could give me. I had to live through His terms to get to understand life and love.

Funny thing, Gary did not know Clarey's real name until they applied for their license. "Who are you?" he

---

[*] The opposite of sadness: a mind full of cucumber boats, warm quilts, yoyos, big fluffy clouds and God, when you notice you are smiling hard

joked as they filled out the license. The clerk of court loved that!

Ann Clarissa Marie O'Brien. But Clarey was not short for Clarissa as everyone thought. I think Dad went along with her nickname because he had chosen her middle name. It was really because she played Sister Clarey in a junior high play at school. Mom and Ceci teased her for a while with the name after the play was over. And it stuck. With her habit still donned, she stood in front of our father. "I thee dubbed Clarey." It was really the only name I knew her by, with twelve years between us.

They had the best married life. I got the cute little O'Brien house to myself when Clarey married Gary. In those five years, I had dabbled in dating but felt I would never have a Gary for myself—I wasn't ready to know how to be loved that much. I was stuck in non-loving myself or my God for a while and it was a pit. Drake, my short-term lover, was deemed a good catch by Clarey, but I couldn't love him loosely. I was holding back all the time with him. I was finally evolving into spirituality again, I could sense it in everything I did or said, in every movement, in other people, but so slowly.

It was almost a juxtaposition, but God became *of* my life. I was welcoming the change, the movement out of the depression. Living alone wasn't so bad. I had time to find myself and my God. This was for me, extremely unlike that love of God I superficially had when I went to novice orientation. That was a learned response to the tapes in my head about being Catholic. This new-found spirituality was full bodied, all encompassing, a turn on, heart rendering, metaphysical tears in a second, living in gratitude and blessedness. Connected through heads and hearts, an inability to feel alone anymore.

It was a big house though and eventually, Barry moved in with me. Combining payments and kitchens just seemed logical, as we were always together. We hung out a lot after Ceci died, so much that he almost lived with me anyway, except for the Drake period. And Barry and I went to a lot of cool places that we had talked about that Ceci and Barry had planned to do someday. Ceci's friends became my closer friends because of our kinship and mourning together and support of one another. They talked about Ceci a lot. It did my heart good, both during the five years of grieving and now P.G.—Post-Grief. And for Ceci's friends and Barry and I to continue making memories did all of our heart's good and seemed to honor Ceci somehow. Now P.G., I felt I had to live life large for my sister, Ceci, and I. Her life had been cut short, so I had to make up a lifetime for two lives. Barry called it my LLL Bean period. Live Life Large. Even bought me a t-shirt with LLL and a picture of a bean on it. He would quote it back to me, "LLL Bean" when he knew I was taking on a new challenge or doing something that Ceci would have done or Ceci had planned to do. If I was experiencing joy, I would offer it for Ceci and really deeply smile inside my own heart, satiated with good feelings.

Barry and I were making up acronyms and nicknames, like he and Cec used to do. Anyway, it began like that... me thinking that I was like Ceci, and then discovering that I was like me.

And at first, living together was still strictly practiced as platonic but made such good financial sense and we were eating together all the time anyway, and it was silly to keep two houses, and, and, and…any other excuses we could find to be together.

It must have been time in our male–female relationship for the next step of bonding since I was definitely now P.G. (that's Post-Grief, remember). He knew first, for sure, that it was love. He sensed it for longer than I knew. He loved me. We had been hand-holding forever. We had kissed on the cheeks always, but of late, we're letting the kiss slip onto the lips and both liking it. Then a knowing lingering look.

Barry and I had hugged a lot and found ourselves passionately kissing a few times, but we hadn't consummated anything. It was time apparently for the next step of bonding.

Living together allowed us to share more than time. Every emotion, every noise, every humdrum moment, every ecstasy, all problems, all needs, sandwiches, and spills. Our characters fit. His fulfillment was my need, his favorites became my treats as well, and my sadness was held in his arms. Life sharing was treasured. We were committed in souls to a grander search of God. Was this love?

He proposed. What was he doing proposing? I know we were exclusive partners to one another for the last number of months, but the time had passed without me really thinking about that. Our petting, I thought came from desire for Barry, but I also saw it as totally selfish on my part. I wanted to be loved and I wanted to love. There is great joy found there. I loved our passion. And my desire was met with equal relish from him. I realized Barry always took care with me, and I told him I loved him for who he was to me and Ceci—the "me" part in that had seemed selfish. I wanted Barry to kiss me but didn't know it. When it happened, his kiss made me feel right in my own world. I realized I did love him like Clarey loved Gary, like my sisters. Wait a minute… That's real close to love, honor, and the joke obey from the wedding vows.

It was at Beartooth Mountain, on one of our cross-country snow ski trips. I was focusing my camera to center the tooth in the lens, and he held up the ring, perfectly encircling the Bear's Tooth in the layout. I snapped the photo. I could prove it to you with a picture. We had come up the pass in early June and stopped at the Continental Divide for a mountain scenery photo op.

"You loved Ceci," I blurted in answer, peering from the camera. I gestured with my hand on my hip like a mother in challenge to her toddlers.

His grin went from ear to ear, the dimples deepening; he was so pleased with himself. "And you!" was his response.

Not the response Shakespeare would have written, but there is no Correct Response School or we would have fewer jerks in the world.

Three hours on-my-finger later, we were out of the mountain pass and Barry had my answer. "Not now" for the wedding, was all that I told him.

He said, "Okay, later. Let me know when." He wasn't mad. It was like, "Let's send out for pizza," "No, let's go Chinese," or "We're out of milk." Like "You'll marry me next week. No big deal that you said no now." In fact, I think that was what I meant. No, as in not this week.

He didn't bring it up the next week though. He waited.

It was me. I was the problem. I always thought of Barry as Ceci's. It is hard to wrap my head around the fact that I loved him for me—not just because Ceci did and he loved her. It is easy to admire someone for loving your sister. I admired Barry—he was good to Ceci and with Ceci. They had an easiness between them. He had been the perfect complement to her persona—they were best friends. So to place myself in the partner-forever mode with Barry was another awakening. I had to step outside of myself to realize what was happening. He was no longer just Ceci's friend that I inherited. He was like a brother but not like a brother. He was supposed to be in my life, there was no doubt about that, but just what was this new role and these feelings?

Maybe our previous petting and kissing and making out had been for us, not just my selfish need to be loved. Not so selfish after all. I wanted to do anything Barry wanted to do. I wanted to see Barry happy. I needed to see Barry happy. I was happy that I did make Barry happy. I was doubly happy when what he did for me made me happy. Wait a minute, that's love and care. Real close to "to have and to hold, to cherish." Real close to wedding vows.

And I realized he wanted me as much. I wanted to calm any worries and hold him when he was bothered, such as he did for me. I wanted to be held by him when I hurt...a bipod hug.

The Bear's Tooth was the perfect sign that we were to marry; after all, the ring was perfectly around the mountain in the photo.

# New Life

CLAREY INVITED ME TO the ultrasound. Turns out Great Uncle Sid (Sidney) had a twin, but Rodney had died at birth, so we discovered as we pursued our genealogy a bit. She had twins in there. We had the gene. There were two heart beats coming from Clarey's belly and now four feet were visible. Yikes. Life would forever be different for Clarey and Gary. I tried not to scream, but my insides were dancing so much I bounded out an excited "Yipes!" Gary jumped up and down with me, arms hooked.

That afternoon, Barry and I took two roses to Ceci's grave. We always had to "share" news with Ceci, and the cemetery was naturally our connector. Strange how you think about all the places you had stood in joy with the deceased, so it is natural to go to the cemetery to talk. It had been cloudy all day till the moment we laid the two flowers down on Ceci's grave. A patch of sunlight broke through the clouds onto the grave and continued to break up the clouds overhead like an earthquake fissure, fighting to take in more and more space in its neon white gold earthen rays. Was Ceci smiling back with her joy for Clarey from the heavens?

Clarey's pregnancy went well. Picture perfect, actually. She wasn't sick, and she was so cute the whole way through. The babies developed perfectly. Wow, bless our hearts.

And Barry and I developed perfectly, now that I was P.G. (Post-Grief) myself and realized that I had fallen in love with Barry while he fell in love with me. I had had no idea about veritable love. Good thing it slipped in naturally. I was too young with my parents to have understood about requited love. Dad had died early in my life, so love was puzzling to me, except for what we sisters had. I was just little and immature to see it in my parents before they left my life. I suppose I subconsciously felt their love. It felt good, whatever it was. And so did this connection with Barry. It felt real good.

I watched Gary and Clarey blossom into their oneness, moving like a unit through life's challenges and excitements, deepened souls when their matching little people came. I could see it because I now understood it. I had a piece of the glory-of-love pie myself.

They didn't need my prayers to be good parents, but I said a novena in the days before the twins were born. I prayed that the twins would know a family like I had with my sisters. And of course, Clarey's room was filled with roses when the babies were born. I had another fulfilled novena! (Okay, so maybe I sent some of the roses!)

Believe it or not, the babies were baptized Marissa Cecilia and Teresa Cecilia. Mari and Teri, oh please, Gary and Clarey!

I don't know if it was the excitement of feeling so like a family, the wonderment of the new lives of the babies or giddiness of being in love, but Barry and I consummated

147

our pledges the night the babies were born, paralleling that babies are consummated the night love is born. I felt all the things were in place. I was experiencing all sorts of things I knew of couples.

I had what Gary and Clarey had, what my parents made me feel, what made our ancestors create wedding vows. I had to develop into a maturity to recognize it in my brain, but my heart had it all along. Barry and I were both in love. We had true love and all of its facets. It was happening to me, things that Ceci had never experienced with Barry. This was my love. This was my time. This was my life for living. We had all that I know love to be. It was now my love, no more loving Barry from Ceci's heart. It was my heart I carried. And my heart in love I was feeling. I wanted to be proposed to again.

Captivated looks, staring into each other's eyes with deeply-shared knowing.

Companionship even when apart in a room

Passionate desire that innately bursts into tight hugs which won't let go

Deep concern for every aspect of the other's happiness

Need for one another's nearness

An ache when not together, for the "missing thing"

Sharing talk

Synchronization in movement, like floating around a room in perfect harmony

Care shining in each other's eyes, visible to anyone looking

Compassion beyond belief—where the heart talks

The "Come here" desire that matches yours and you respond to

Gentle thoughtfulness in all ways, servile love

Tenderness in thought

Tenderness with each other's bodies

Alike values that go deep—spending, care, concern, causes, and beliefs

Playfulness

Bringing back two cokes when you didn't ask

Sharing suppositions, even about Heaven or God

A blanket before you are just about to feel the chill

Affectionate touching

Beside-ness

Nestling without a twitch for hours

Knowing attachment even when apart

Sharing truth only

Constant flirtatious banter

Excitement between our hearts, evident when you walk in a room

Knowing their bowel habits

Common likes

Carpal tunnel empty feeling when he is not here to hold my hand

Knowing and loving the way their body smells, even sweaty

Sweetness that causes pause

Pet names

Knowing glances

Fights that have no intention of harm

Awesome cherish-ocity

Feeling nothing when another person comes on to you

Wanting their exploration of your body

And wanting to explore every pore of them

Supportive words and looks above any

Fingers searching one another's hand to hold without looking

Polite consideration

Please and thank you

An ache for that sense of his flesh touching yours

Smelling them on you after lovemaking

Twined feet in bed with toes touching just because

Panties from the laundry on his head

Calmness in the feel of his warm breath on you

Spirited play

> You call his mom/he calls your grandma
> Connected souls in a room full of strangers
> Noticeable protection
> Devotion
> Understanding,
> Generosity
> Tuned in to needs
> Respect
> Nicknames
> Okay, and to sometimes "obey"

And that ever-endearing term, honor.

I came across the Bear's Tooth picture and playfully stuck it in the bathroom mirror for Barry to find. He came back and kissed my ring finger without saying a word.

"Come on," I told him after breakfast. "We have somewhere to go." I stopped at the florist and got a single rose. One rose to convey what we wanted to share with Ceci. And we went to the cemetery. The caretaker was weed-whacking on the far side of the grounds, his truck near Ceci's plot. As we walked up to her rectangle, still identifiably new grave after five years, we saw two empty weed-whacker spools, lying as if rings intertwined at Ceci's foot. She had already got the word.

Clarey let Barry and I babysit soon after the babies were born. We had been dying to babysit, but we nearly had to force Gary and Clarey to go out for dinner. We couldn't wait to have the girls to ourselves. Barry brought home with him a potted rosebush that night. He said that we needed to plant roses at our house, so that we would have the happiness my Novenas brought all the time. It was a good sign.

Barry and I were each holding one of Clarey's sleeping babies, having rocked them simultaneously into slumber. He reached out his hand with a palm toward me. "Now?" he asked.

"Now," I said.

I may go to my grave with a tiny bit in me thinking that Barry married me because I was like Ceci. But what greater tribute to my sister could he offer? And for me, my aspirations were always to be like her. And so it was. A nebulous tripod, hearts locked in hearts, death do us not part.

Have you written a letter to God recommending yourself to be let into heaven?

Sit down. Right now. I'll start it for you…

From the King of Earth to God:

I want to tell you about (fill in your name) Jean.

# About the Author

JEAN POSUSTA, ON HER fifth adventure of comedic and novel fiction, *I see You with My Heart* frankly addresses one of society's secret sufferings—death of a loved one. *I see You with My Heart* cuts through the clouds, bluntly putting thoughts of great fear and great love onto printed page. Emotional edges throughout. Posusta has authored murder mysteries for performance, song lyrics for music teachers, and self-help literature, after her journalism stint for various periodicals. *Twisted Winds of Verango* and *Hope We Don't Go to Paulette's Again Soon* are among her other publications and printings.

*I see You with My Heart* is evocative and deceptively intuitive, cuts through the clouds.

CPSIA information can be obtained
at www.ICGtesting.com
Printed in the USA
BVHW081126020220
571059BV00001B/5